NINETY YEARS OF THI
RAMSEY STEAMSHIP C(

Edward Gray and Roy Fenton

A Ships in Focus Fleet History

Published in the UK in 2003 by Ships in Focus Publications,
18 Franklands, Longton
Preston PR4 5PD

Printed by Amadeus Press Ltd., Cleckheaton, West Yorkshire
ISBN 1-901703-50-9

Cover: *Ben Varrey* (4) arrives in the Isle of Man for the first time. *[Company archives]*
Back cover: Flag and funnel of the Ramsey Steamship Co. Ltd. *[J.L. Loughran]*
         Ben Ain (1) at Douglas. *[A.S. Breeze, courtesy David Woodward]*
Title page: *Ben Varrey* (1). *[Douglas Cochrane, World Ship Photo Library]*

FOREWORD

To attain the age of ninety is a significant achievement. To do so as a coastal shipping company is even more notable; and to do so while retaining the same independent, private company status, with no takeovers or calls for additional funding is quite possibly unique.

The Directors of the Ramsey Steamship Company were pleased to be asked by Mr Roy Fenton to co-operate with Mr Ted Gray in the compilation of this book to record the history of the Company. It is a difficult task to condense ninety years into a book of this size and we are indebted to Mr Gray for having accomplished this so effectively.

Captain J.T. Kee, who was a retired sailing ship master and the driving force in the flotation of the Company, would be proud indeed to see how his initiative and enterprise had flourished. Most of the original shares are still held by the descendants of the founding members.

That the Company has survived through times, which have included many more periods of turbulent rather than smooth trading conditions, is due in no small part to the dedication and determination of the five successive, long serving, managers and loyal, hard working, Captains, crew and office staff. The shareholders, by being satisfied with modest returns, have also played their part.

A theme which has run through the Board Room down the years is the now fashionable word, prudence. During the few buoyant periods the temptation for rapid expansion has been resisted and a policy of prudence and consolidation been followed. This may lead to an unspectacular way of business life, but it has been a recipe for survival and continued secure employment for successive generations of seafarers.

Captain Ramsey Cringle, Chairman of the Ramsey Steamship Co. Ltd.

Above: Ben Ain (1) at Douglas, along with a circus, 3rd September 1956. [*World Ship Photo Library*]

Opposite: *Ben Veg* (2) hits rough weather immediately she leaves Douglas harbour on 26th January 1966. [*Stan Basnett*]

ACKNOWLEDGEMENTS

Managing Director Tony Kennish generously allowed access to the company's minute books, cargo books, and other miscellaneous papers and records in the Douglas offices, and answered many queries about the day-to-day workings of the business. We are also grateful to Marine Superintendent Chris van Buul and to Mark Bumfrey. Captain Ramsey Cringle kindly took time to answer questions about the founders and their families. Files of Dissolved Companies in the care of the Manx Museum were consulted for details of the Island Steamship Company. Adrian Corkill is the author of the 'Dictionary of Shipwrecks off the Isle of Man' and has located two of the sunken vessels. Previously published short histories of the company are by Michael B. Wray (in 'Maritime History' 1973) and A.M. Goodwyn (in 'Manx Transport Review' 1987). J.I.C. Boyd's history of 'The Isle of Man Railway' (Oakwood Press, 1994) provided details of the harbour tramway. Thanks to Alan Palmer for the map of the tramway, and to Stan Basnett for assistance in tracing illustrations.

Especial gratitude is due to Edward Paget Tomlinson, who has been involved since the idea of a published history of the company first germinated, and who has been highly supportive throughout.

Photographers whose work has been used are acknowledged in the captions, but special mention must be made of the negative collection of John Clarkson, without which the book would have been much the poorer. Thanks also to Tony Kennish who facilitated the use of photographs in the company's possession. Also to be particularly thanked are Stan Basnett, John Cowley, Keith Byass, David Woodward, and those involved with the World Ship Society's Photo Library - Tony Smith, Jim McFaul and David Whiteside - and those photographers no longer with us who created some of the images, including George Osbon, Douglas Cochrane and A.S. Breeze. Louis Loughran kindly provided the flag and funnel illustration for the back cover.

The fleet lists have benefited from the input of a number of researchers, including Gil Mayes, David Burrell, Ron Evans, Bill Harvey and the late Rowan Hackman. Use of the resources of the World Ship Society's Merchant Ship Collections, the help of Anne Cowne of the Information Section of Lloyd's Register of Shipping, the Guildhall Library, and the Public Record Office is gratefully acknowledged.

If, in the lengthy gestation of this publication, any deserving names have been omitted, apologies are offered.

NOTES ON THE FLEET LISTS

The ships' histories are in chronological order according to the completion date of new ships or of acquisition. The notation '1' or '2' in brackets after a ship's name indicates that she is the first or second ship of that name in the fleet where the name has been used more than once. The dates following the name are those of entering and leaving the company ownership or management. Unless otherwise stated vessels are steel screw steamers.

On the first line is given the ship's British official number followed by her tonnages, gross (g) and net (n) at the time of acquisition. Dimensions given are the registered length x breadth x depth at the time of acquisition expressed in decimal feet or metres for vessels built after 1965.

On the following line is a description of the engines fitted and the name of their builder. Steam engines may be two-cylinder compounds (C. 2-cyl.), or three-cylinder triple-expansion (T. 3-cyl.). For oil engines are given the type (e.g. Brons), the number of cylinders, whether two stroke (2SC) or four stroke (4SC) cycle, single acting (SA) or double acting (DA). Figures for horsepower are nominal (NHP), indicated horsepower (IHP) and brake horsepower (BHP). Nominal horsepower bears least relationship to the engine's actual power, but is often the only figure available. Speeds are taken from registration documents, and are usually estimated not trial's figures. Changes to the engines are listed, with dates, on subsequent lines.

For ships whose British register was closed before 1955, careers under British ownership and technical details have been derived from registration documents in class BT110 in the Public Records Office, Kew.

THE RAMSEY STEAMSHIP CO. LTD.

The port of Ramsey

The harbour at Ramsey, on the north-east coast of the Isle of Man, lies at the mouth of the Sulby, the island's longest river. Ramsey Bay has long been known as a safe anchorage for vessels sheltering from storms. In the nineteenth century, Ramsey was the principal port for the export of grain, whilst imported goods came mainly via Whitehaven, only 35 miles from Ramsey, or Liverpool. The island had no natural supplies of coal, so this became a principal import, particularly from the Cumberland coalfield through Whitehaven to Ramsey. (Ramsey was also early noted for the import of contraband goods. Indeed, it was alleged that the main occupation was smuggling, hence the early development of a Ramsey coastguard station.) In the 1850s the Ramsey-based vessel *Manx Fairy* competed briefly with the larger and better-known Isle of Man Steam Packet Company for Liverpool traffic. At this time, too, a flourishing shipbuilding industry was burgeoning, and the harbour was one of three (the others being at Douglas and Peel) improved by an Act of Tynwald in 1861. Ore from the island's developing mining industry was carried to coastal ports in horse-drawn carts. On the return journey the carts carried coal. Roads were poor, and the opening of the Isle of Man Railway from Douglas to Peel in 1873 and to Port Erin in 1874 offered a more efficient means of distributing coal in the south of the island. The north of the island was excluded from the first railway plans, but it was not long before the Manx Northern Railway completed a line from St. John's to Ramsey (1879) and shortly afterwards gained permission to extend the track from the terminus along the quayside to permit the discharge of coal direct from ship into railway wagons. The importance of this 1883 extension, known as the Harbour Tramway, was further increased when rail connection was made from St. John's to the Foxdale lead mines in 1887. Thereafter, traffic in lead ore to Ramsey for shipment outwards, and inward traffic in coal for the mines, the railway, and other users, became the principal purpose of the harbour tramway. Strangely, a similar proposal by the Isle of Man Railway Company for a rail connection along the North Quay at Douglas harbour was never achieved, giving Ramsey an undoubted advantage in the matter of trans-shipment of coal, until the ubiquitous motor lorry came on the scene some 40 years later.

In the early years of the twentieth century, two days were required to unload a cargo of 200 tons of coal at Ramsey. The coal was shovelled into tubs, which were then hoisted to the quayside. (Using today's mechanical aids, 1,000 tons can be unloaded in one day.) The harbour tramway had three short sidings off the main line, and wagons could be left alongside the ship's berth. When filled, the wagons would be assembled into a train for hauling along the quay to join the railway proper at Ramsey Station. The export of ore had all but vanished before the First World War as production dwindled and the mines closed, but imports of coal remained at a high level. As Ramsey was the only Isle of Man port connected to the railway system, all railway coal arrived here for distribution to locomotive depots in Peel, Port Erin, and even Douglas.

Origins of the Ramsey Steamship Co. Ltd.

The story of the Ramsey Steamship Company is very much bound-up with the Kee family. Captain John Thomas Kee (1854-1926) was the son of a Ramsey blacksmith, whose work included commissions for the Ramsey shipyard. John Thomas Kee did not follow his father's trade, but went to sea and eventually became master of sailing ships, trading world-wide for the Liverpool-based enterprise of William Lowden and Company, a connection which was to recur later in his son's business ventures. At the close of his seafaring career, John Thomas Kee established a coal merchant's business on Ramsey quay, in which he was joined by his son John Brown Kee (1883-1934).

It was a natural development of their enterprise that, in the process of importing huge quantities of coal, they began to consider the advantages of owning their own steamer to bring in cargoes at more favourable rates. Accordingly, they assembled a group of Ramsey businessmen with the object of acquiring one or more small steamships to trade between the Isle of Man, chiefly Ramsey, and ports on the mainland. Those involved in the scheme with John Thomas Kee were Frederick Brew (banker), Robert Brew (grocer), Alfred Christian (farmer), Thomas Baker Cowley (corn merchant), John William Hyde (advocate), and Robert Evan Kennish (corn merchant). The proposed venture attracted considerable local support and, on the 26th April 1913, the Ramsey Steamship Co. Ltd. came into being, with an authorised capital of £4,200

The Ramsey Quay Tramway was constructed in 1882-83 when the Manx Northern Railway Company extended its track from the station precincts (site of the present Ramsey Bakery) across Bowring Road and along Derby Road to serve steamer berths on West Quay. A proposed further extension along East Quay was never built. The easternmost track and siding opposite Market Place was removed in 1924-25, but the remainder continued in use until 1951. The track was removed in 1954-57. *[Alan Palmer].*

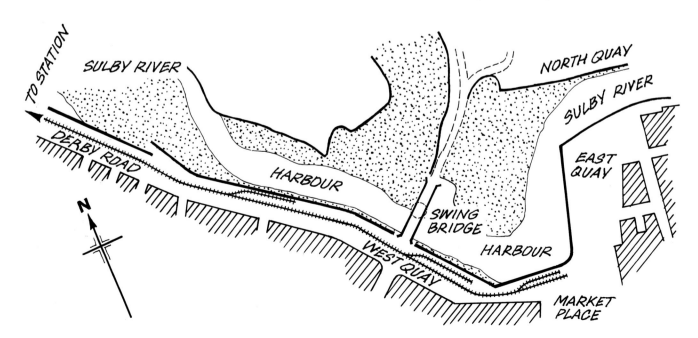

Isle of Man Railway 2-4-0T No. 8 *Fenella* on Ramsey Quay. *[T.H. Midwood, courtesy Stan Basnett]*

in £1 shares. On the 19th May 1913, the signatories to the Memorandum and Articles of Association met at 'The Courier' newspaper offices in Parliament Street, Ramsey, appointed Robert Brew as Chairman, and agreed that J.T. Kee's son, John Brown Kee, should be Secretary and Manager, with the registered office of the new company at 25 West Quay.

The founders jointly could muster sufficient trade for their own businesses to justify the purchase of a vessel, and any additional freight over and above their own requirements would represent profit. They calculated that a steamship could make two-and-a-half trips across to the mainland each week, or nine per month. The current freight rate from Garston to Ramsey was quoted at four shillings to four-shillings-and-three-pence per ton, which, the prospectus claimed, 'allows for a drop to 3/6 on 150 tons per trip.' For insurance purposes, it was agreed that trading would be limited to the north Irish Sea, that is between Londonderry and the River Clyde as a northern boundary, and between Bardsey Island in Wales and Arklow on the east coast of Ireland as a southern boundary.

At first, the purchase of a second-hand vessel was mooted (the 18-year-old *Glentow* (159/1895) and the 19-year-old *Ardgowan* (185/1894) were considered), but eventually the partners decided on a completely new vessel, built to order by the Larne Shipbuilding Company, Northern Ireland, at a cost of £4,089-13s-6d. The new ship completed in August 1914 was a coaster of 159 gross tonnage, captained by John Cowley, and named *Ben Veg* (Manx Gaelic for 'Little Woman'), thus commencing a naming policy which continues to the present day. The *Ben Veg's* maiden voyage was on the 17th August 1914, when she carried a cargo of stone to Liverpool. Other bulk cargoes of sand, cement, salt, and, of course, coal, were soon forthcoming, so that at the first Annual General Meeting of the company in October 1914, held at Corlett's Tea Rooms, Ramsey, the mood was celebratory.

Ben Veg (1), the company's first steamer.
[T.H. Midwood, courtesy John Cowley]

An interesting view of two of the company's early steamers, *Ben Rein* (1) and aft of her *Whitestone*, later to become *Ben Varrey* (1). The photograph must have been taken between June 1917, when *Whitestone* was bought from Glasgow owners, and February 1918, when *Ben Rein* was sunk by a German submarine. Despite it being wartime, neither ship is in grey, but in full company livery. The location is the inner harbour at Ramsey, with the chimney of the salt works visible. [*John Cowley collection*]

Trevor, second steamer of the Douglas Shipping Co. Ltd. [*J. and M. Clarkson*]

Wartime conditions, 1914-1918

The early years of the company's operations coincided with the onset of wartime conditions and an immediate increase in trade, which led the founders to consider the purchase of a second vessel. Certain problems of 'leakage' had been experienced with the *Ben Veg*, which the company alleged was due to defective workmanship. Repairs had cost £70, which the company tried to reclaim from the Larne Shipbuilding Company. The latter offered £27, which was accepted with reluctance. A bid to buy the steamship *Isabel* for £2,700 failed. The purchase of a new vessel at this period was out of the question, as all

yards were busy with wartime requirements, but suitable second-hand ships were hard to find.

At the second Annual General Meeting in 1915, a dividend of 5% was declared. Shortly afterwards, a set-back occurred when the *Ben Veg*, leaving Garston with a cargo of coal for Peel, collided with the steam flat *Britannia* in the River Mersey off Herculaneum Dock. To the dismay of the directors, it was discovered that the company was insured only for damage done, and not for damage received.

The increased demand for shipping during the war years resulted in a rise in freight rates. The profits to be gained were such as to recover investment rapidly. By 1916 the rate for cartage of coal from a place such as the Partington Coaling Basin, on the Manchester Ship Canal, to Ramsey was eight shillings per ton, but the Secretary was authorised to accept seven shillings on condition that the vessel could be discharged 'in twelve running hours.' The search for a second vessel continued, and in July 1916 the steamship *Starling* was on offer for inspection at Liverpool. Purchase was agreed, the ship subsequently being renamed *Ben Rein*. Captain Cowley was transferred from the *Ben Veg* to take over the newly-acquired vessel, which was eleven years old and somewhat larger than the first ship. Initially, it seemed to be a bad buy, for 'considerable engine room trouble' was reported. However, this was solved satisfactorily, and a dividend of 6% was declared for the year ending in September 1916.

The quick profits available in this troubled period encouraged competitors to enter the business. One such was the Douglas Shipping Co. Ltd., formed in 1916 to trade between Irish Sea ports. Its founders were two Lancashire and three Manx businessmen, one of latter being George Kelly, harbourmaster at Douglas, who became the managing director.

The Douglas Shipping Company first traded briefly but profitably with three small sailing ships, and was soon financially sound enough to move into steam, which it did in 1917 acquiring the 1884-built *Texa* from David MacBrayne, and a second steamship, the *Trevor*, in 1919.

This new competition did not affect the activities of the Ramsey Steamship Company. The war years brought more business than expected, and early in 1917 the purchase of a third vessel, the steamship *Whitestone*, owned by Archibald Robertson of Glasgow, was considered at the price of £12,000. Possibly the *Ben Rein* was still giving trouble, for at the same time a proposal for the disposal of this vessel was discussed, the directors estimating that its sale might raise some £10,000. In the event, the *Whitestone* was purchased in June 1917, ultimately to be renamed *Ben Varrey*, but not until two years later. Still as *Whitestone*, under Captain E. Jones from the

Ben Veg, she was immediately placed on a six-month charter to Watt and Sons, of Portrush, Northern Ireland, whilst the *Ben Rein* was retained and continued with her usual sailings until lost by enemy action on the 7th February 1918. Whilst on passage from Liverpool to Belfast with a cargo of soap, the sound of gunfire was heard, and, as the haze lifted, crew members on deck saw the Liverpool steamer *Limesfield* (427/ 1916) of the Zillah Shipping Co. Ltd. under attack by the German submarine *UB 57*. The *Ben Rein* put on speed to try to escape, but, having sunk the *Limesfield*, the submarine gave chase and ordered the *Ben Rein* to stop. A lifeboat was launched and pulled clear before the *UB 57* sank the *Ben Rein* by gunfire 35 miles north west of the Liverpool Bar. The crew of seven were picked up by the coaster *Norman* and landed at Whitehaven the following day. The directors agreed to send the sum of ten guineas to be shared amongst the crew of the *Norman* as an expression of thanks for their assistance in saving the crew of the *Ben Rein* and for their kindness to the survivors at Whitehaven.

Thus reduced to two ships once again, the search resumed for additional tonnage, though costs were rising steeply due to wartime inflation. The *Redstone*, another Robertson steamer, became available in October 1918, and the directors agreed after inspection to negotiate from a price of £16,500 or less, 'less the best allowance obtainable for bottom damage.' She was duly acquired, and in July 1919 was renamed *Ben Vooar*. Shortly before this renaming, another vessel had been purchased. This fourth member of the fleet was the small steamship *Tern*, which was renamed to become the second *Ben Rein*.

Ben Rein (2), added in June 1919, was destined to have only a two-year spell in the Ramsey fleet. Possibly she proved unsatisfactory in some way, or perhaps she was considered too small, but her disposal was being considered as early as March 1920, when the company hoped to receive £10,250 from her sale. At this time, the company had agreed the purchase of a new ship, under construction as the *Deveson* (though never registered in this name) at the Ellesmere Port yard of the Manchester Dry Docks Company. The original prospective buyers were reportedly declared insolvent, so the new vessel was completed in May 1920 as the *Ben Seyr*. The Manchester Dry Docks Company was noted more as a repairer of ships than a shipbuilder, but in the early 1920s four small coasters were constructed at Ellesmere Port, two of which had originally been ordered by the wartime Shipping Controller, and the materials for two more had been placed in stock by the yard. The depressed state of the trade in post-

A delightful view of *Whitestone*. *[John Cowley collection]*

war years accounts for the delay in completion, the *Ben Seyr* being the first of the four (Yard Nos. 71 - 74) to leave the stocks, making her first voyage to Ramsey with a cargo of coal on the 22nd May 1920. In passing, it is worth noting that two more of these four vessels would enter the Ramsey fleet in later years.

The insurance values of the fleet in 1920 are of interest. In descending order they were:

Ben Seyr	£19,000
Ben Vooar	£16,500
Ben Varrey	£15,000
Ben Veg	£10,000
Ben Rein (2)	£ 8,000

A dividend of 10% was declared in 1920, but a troubled period loomed ahead, as freight rates collapsed. In the following year, the directors voted not to pay an interim dividend in order to 'conserve resources' and some ships were laid up for a period from 1st April 1921 as a result of the general strike of coal miners on the mainland. An offer of £4,500 (less £250 agent's commission) was accepted for the *Ben Rein* (2), and she left the fleet in October 1921.

The Island Steamship Company, 1923

The unsettled period following the 1914-1918 war may seem to have been an unlikely time to commence a new enterprise, but three members of the Ramsey Steamship board, namely the then chairman Frederick Brew, manager John Brown Kee, and his father, director John Thomas Kee, purchased the converted steam drifter *Lord Milner* from the Admiralty. The *Lord Milner* first appeared in Ramsey in February 1922 carrying a cargo of coal from Cardiff, and then went to Port St. Mary to have a winch fitted. In the short time she was owned in Ramsey, the *Lord Milner* was employed mainly in importing petroleum in casks to Douglas, though inward cargoes of coal and outward of salt are recorded. J.B. Kee managed the ship separately, but alongside, his work for the Ramsey Steamship Company, with the knowledge and approval of the other directors. However, the results must not have been satisfactory. At a meeting on the 21st April 1922 her three owners offered the *Lord Milner* to the Ramsey Steamship Company 'at cost.' The interested parties were asked to retire from the meeting, whilst the other directors considered the offer, which was declined as being 'out of line' with the rest of the company's tonnage. The Ramsey Steamship Company directors added that they were 'perfectly satisfied that the operation of this steamer has not in any way been against the interests of this company and have confidence in the owners' assurance that no traffic will be accepted for their vessel which could advantageously be carried by one of the company's steamers.' The vessel was, in fact, sold in January 1924.

In the following year John Brown Kee and Frederick Brew, assisted this time by director Thomas Baker Cowley, began a second side-venture when they formed the Island Steamship Co. Ltd. in May 1923. The company's first ship proper, the *Pembrey*, was bought from A.H. Connell of Liverpool for £7,500, making its first voyage for the company on 15th June 1923. (Connell had only recently acquired the vessel from the Burryside Steamship Co. Ltd., Burry

Port, Llanelly, South Wales.) The new company intended the *Pembrey* to trade between English ports and ports of Northern France, but freight rates fell, trade was depressed, and the vessel evidently operated at a loss. In fact, the Island Steamship Company arranged only two cargoes for the *Pembrey* whilst nominally working the vessel.

In October 1923 A.H. Connell, from whom the *Pembrey* had been purchased, joined the new company as a fellow director, as did J.C. Brew. Alfred Herbert Connell was a principal of Lowden, Connell and Company, Liverpool shippers. His father Robert Lowden Connell was nephew of William Lowden, for whom John Thomas Kee had sailed years earlier, and his company already had an interest in the island in the shape of the Manx Isles Steamship Co. Ltd. formed in 1905.

A.H. Connell became the largest shareholder in the Island Steamship Company, with 500 shares, followed by Frederick Brew with 450, and J.B. Kee with 350. His Liverpool firm, Lowden, Connell and Company, took over arrangements for running the *Pembrey*, which was being

The converted trawler *Lord Milner* at the Preston yard of T.W. Ward Ltd. Sold to the scrap merchant in 1924, she was used to carry scrap between yards. *[World Ship Photo Library]*

offered for sale in a falling market as early as the winter of 1923. However, a buyer offering a reasonably acceptable price could not be found. Thereafter, Lowden, Connell and Company managed the vessel, sending remittances from time to time as a result of the business arranged by them. The ship did, in fact, work to Northern France, Belgium, and the Channel Isles, but was laid up after the summer of 1925 and again the following year, trade being unprofitable. It was noted that 'the state of the Continental market is such that she can only run at a loss.' The ship was sold to a Belgian buyer in 1928.

The Island Steamship Company had greater success carrying bulk cargoes (mainly coal) in smaller vessels working between Irish Sea ports. The *Lyd*, a small iron dandy, was acquired in December 1923 (but sold after twelve months), whilst the *Staffa* operated from 1925 to 1930. The *Fawn* (bought 1927) was found to be unsuitable for the coal trade because of her small hatch and derrick, and was almost exclusively employed in carrying petroleum in casks from Liverpool to Douglas and returning with empties, with the

Uniquely amongst the company's vessels, the second *Ben Rein* kept her Ramsey name after her sale in 1921, and retained it under various owners until her loss in 1941. Here she still carries sails. *[Roy Fenton collection]*

occasional additional cargoes of the weekend 'Sunday Dispatch' newspapers for the island.

The Island Steamship Company ceased trading in 1930, and was subsequently dissolved. Its remaining ship, the *Fawn*, was taken over by another new company, J.B. Kee (1930) Ltd., and sailed on until 1940.

The Ramsey Steamship Company in the 1920s
John Brown Kee continued to manage the Ramsey Steamship Company affairs in tandem with his work for the Island Steamship Company. After the sale of *Ben Rein* (2) in 1921, the fleet was reduced to four until February 1923, when the 1891-built *Sarah Blanche* was acquired and renamed *Ben Blanche*. In the following year, a sixth ship joined the fleet in April 1924 on the purchase of the *Jolly Basil*, which became

Ben Blanche, added to the fleet in 1923. [J. and M. Clarkson collection]

Ben Jee (1) bunkering at Preston. *[J. and M. Clarkson]*

Ben Jee. Despite this increase in activities, things were not well, and in June 1924 the directors held a lengthy debate on the state of the coasting trade. In March 1926, matters were such that the directors agreed to waive half their fee '…in the interests of the Company.'

Problems were compounded when the Lancashire and Yorkshire Bank, which had held the company's funds since its inception, refused to recognise the security offered by the company's assets. The directors decided to 'seek accommodation elsewhere,' and found the Isle of Man Bank more amenable.

The period of depression was made worse by the onset of the 1926 General Strike. The first effect felt by the company was on the 3rd May 1926, when the *Ben Seyr* put into Waterford to replenish her bunkers. To the master's dismay, supplies were refused. The crew had to be paid off, but remained with the vessel, unable to return home because of the strike. The *Ben Vooar* was at Londonderry on the same day, but was able to make for Ramsey. The *Ben Blanche* was in Douglas for boiler scaling and the fitting of a new winch and propeller, whilst the *Ben Veg* and *Ben Jee* were laid up at Ramsey on their return to the port. The *Ben Varrey* was able to continue sailing intermittently, the crew being paid off between voyages, and the *Ben Seyr* ultimately arrived in Ramsey to be laid up.

It was during the 1926 General Strike that J.B. Kee's entrepreneurial instincts led him in a new direction. From being an importer of coal, he extended his operations to become an exporter of gravel. A concrete barge, the *Burscough*, was sunk at the Point of Ayre, in the north of the island, to form the basis of a makeshift jetty at which steamers could moor to take on supplies of gravel, abundant in that part of the island.

J.B. Kee arranged his first cargo of gravel for the *Ben Varrey* on the 4th May 1926 and for *Ben Blanche* on the 13th May, after which the latter vessel was laid up, but several similar cargoes were arranged for the *Ben Vooar* and the *Ben Seyr* in July and August. Trade began to pick up again after the summer of 1926, but the *Ben Jee* remained idle until October.

In November 1926 the *Ben Jee* and the *Ben Seyr* began

what was to prove a regular source of revenue for the company when they sailed on time charter for Irish Lights, carrying supplies to the various lighthouses around the coast of Ireland. The *Ben Jee* was chartered from 8th November at a rate of £450 per month, and was returned to Ellesmere Port on the 13th December. The smaller *Ben Seyr* cost £335 per month. Another lengthy charter in 1928, first for three, and then for an additional four months, was that of the *Ben Vooar* at £9-17s-3d per day to Corlett and Cowley to carry drinking water.

The 1920s saw the demise of several coastal traders, but the Ramsey Steamship Company survived by means of shrewd and efficient management to increase its fleet to its maximum of seven vessels with the purchase of the 1894 steamer *Glenmay* (renamed *Ben May*) for £550 in 1928.

The 1930s

By the time of the 16th Annual General Meeting held in February 1930, matters had improved sufficiently for the bank to report that the company was in a 'comfortable position' when compared with that of other coasting companies. The import of coal still accounted for some 75% of the company's traffic, with cargoes of potatoes, oats, manure, flour, maize, ore, cement, tar, alumina, and gravel making up most of the rest. The company which had reported a loss in 1926, and which had seen dividends dwindle to 3%, was now able to declare a dividend of 6%.

Throughout 1931 and 1932 the fleet remained at a total of seven vessels. In 1931 a dividend of 5% was declared, and J.B. Kee was made a director in his own right, but in the slump of 1932 there was no dividend, and the directors waived their fees. Others were faring even worse. The rival Douglas Shipping Co. Ltd., which had already ceased trading, was wound up on the 23rd April 1933 with assets totalling £1,642, which figure included £590 from the sale of its two steamships, *Texa* and *Trevor* the previous year. However, Leonard Callow, who had become manager of the Douglas Shipping Company following the death of George Kelly, continued in business as a ship broker under his own name. The Lloyd's Agency had passed to J.B. Kee in Ramsey, with Leonard Callow appointed sub-agent in Douglas, where, from offices

Ben Seyr, a name used just once. *[John Cowley collection]*

on the North Quay, he acted for most owners calling at the port, with the exception of the Isle of Man Steam Packet Company.

During the depression of 1933 the *Ben Jee* was sold, and on the 17th December the *Ben Blanche* was declared a total loss after running aground in dense fog at Oxwich Head, South Wales. Bound from Dundrum to Swansea with a cargo of potatoes in sacks, the vessel struck rocks and began to take on water. Distress flares were sent up, and the crew took to the two ship's boats, being picked up some hours later by the Mumbles Lifeboat. Two days later, the rescued seamen were entertained to a Christmas party at the Mission

The *veteran Ben May*, 34 years old when acquired in 1928. *[J. and M. Clarkson]*

Ben Vooar (1) of 1916 (above) was wrecked on West Pier, Castlerock at the entrance to the River Bann in June 1936 (below). She was just one of several casualties at this point in the late 1930s. A crane working on obviously much-needed improvements to the Bann entrance can be seen on the breakwater. *[Upper: T.H. Midwood, courtesy John Cowley; lower: Company archives.]*

to Seamen Institute in Swansea, and later that evening left for their homes in the Isle of Man, their tickets being provided by the Mission. Their vessel was later cut up and removed for scrap. J.B. Kee was asked to purchase a suitable steamer to replace the *Ben Blanche* at a sum not exceeding £1,200.

At the 20th Annual General Meeting held in February 1934, the company gained a new Chairman, John William Hyde, as Frederick Brew, a founder, had died. Continuity was provided by John Brown Kee, but, sadly, not for long, for he died in May 1934 at the age of 50. He had been Secretary and Manager of the company since its inception in 1913, a member of Ramsey Town Commissioners, Honorary Secretary for the Ramsey Lifeboat, Lloyd's Agent for the Isle of Man, and had interests in the entertainment and leisure business in the island. His death at such an early age robbed the community of an active and greatly-respected figure. His company, J.B. Kee (1930) Ltd., had taken over the assets of the Island Steamship Company, principally the steamship *Fawn*, and a second vessel, the *Bradda*, had been added in 1930. Both were still trading at the time of his death.

The directors appointed James Ramsay, J.B. Kee's assistant, to be Secretary and Manager at a salary of £4-10s-0d per week. It was agreed that the company would continue to run its own affairs together with those of J.B. Kee (1930) Ltd., for which services J.B. Kee (1930) Ltd. would pay £100 per annum in management fees. The company minutes record: "Mr. Ramsay is to give his attention to J.B. Kee management as well as to this Company," and add the condition that J.B. Kee (1930) Ltd. 'is not to buy any more ships or extend its operations without the written consent of this Company.'

In December 1934 the recession was still biting. The *Ben Blanche* had not been replaced and the fleet was reduced to five. Economies were needed. A reduction in the crew numbers for *Ben Vooar* and *Ben Seyr* was discussed. For the latter, it was agreed that the fireman could be dispensed with, and that an ordinary seaman at a wage of £2 per week could replace a more costly able seaman. For the *Ben Vooar*, it was proposed that the services of an able seaman should be dispensed with altogether, without replacement, and that in his stead the fireman should assist on deck when entering or leaving port, and at other times as required. The engineer's salary was to be reduced from £4-0s-0d to £3-16s-6d, and the masters' salaries on all steamers was to be reduced by fifteen shillings per week

For James Ramsay, dealing with the J.B. Kee (1930) Ltd. operation, the year 1936 started badly with the loss of the

Bradda in January, when it capsized in the River Mersey during a gale. Five of her six crew were lost. Following the loss of this vessel, and presumably with the approval of the Ramsey Steamship Company directors, Ramsay set about finding replacement tonnage, and in May purchased the *Mona's Belle* from an Isle of Man owner, renaming her *J.B. Kee*. The main company, too, had a problem. On the 21st June 1936 the *Ben Vooar* was wrecked at Castlerock whilst heading for Coleraine, fortunately with no loss of life. It was agreed, subject to inspection, to offer £2,750 (with the possibility of an increase to £3,000) for the *Pegrix*, which was duly acquired (for £3,000) to become the *Ben Ellan*.

As trading conditions revived, in 1937 the company was able to offer a modest increase in salaries to partially compensate for the reductions of 1934. The masters' wages were increased by five shillings per week, and the Managing Secretary by one pound. An offer of £2,850 for the steamship *Coombe Dingle* (261/1910) came to nothing. In August 1937 the elderly *Ben May* was sold to a Belfast owner for £380. At the end of the year, at the 24th Annual General Meeting, a dividend of 5% was declared, a level which was maintained for the next three years.

The need for additional tonnage to replace *Ben May* was satisfied temporarily in June 1938 when an offer of £4,050 for the steamship *Cargan* was accepted by her owners, the Larne Steamship Company. She duly entered the fleet to become *Ben Vooar* (2). But disaster struck again with the loss of the *Ben Seyr*, which left Ramsey on Sunday 2nd October 1938 with a cargo of oats for Cardiff. A severe south-westerly gale blew up, and reports suggested that the vessel had sheltered in Rosslare Bay, County Wexford, to ride out the storm, leaving Rosslare on the 5th October to resume her journey to Cardiff, where she would have expected to arrive the next day. But, in fact, she was never seen again. The body of her mate, James Bradford, was later washed up at Middleton Sands near Heysham, leading to speculation that the *Ben Seyr* either foundered soon after leaving Ramsey, or that after leaving Rosslare, the fierce gale had driven the vessel back towards the Isle of Man. The suggestion that the ship was lost soon after leaving Ramsey is supported by the fact that James Bradford's body was still clothed in his best Sunday suit, as if he had taken the helm before changing into his working overalls.

In 1936, *Mona's Belle* was bought by J.B. Kee and Co. Ltd. from owners in Port St. Mary and renamed *J.B. Kee* in honour of this company's founder, who had died in 1934. *[Roy Fenton collection]*

The *Dennis Head*, a sister ship to the *Ben Seyr*, and one of the four built by the Manchester Dry Docks Company at Ellesmere Port, became available in December and was purchased for £3,925. She was re-named *Ben Ain*, bringing the fleet total back to five. A sign of changing times was the company's decision to grant £25 per annum towards the upkeep of the Manager's motor car.

The Second World War
At the outbreak of war in 1939 the company's fleet of five vessels consisted of the original *Ben Veg* of 1914, now 25 years old; *Ben Varrey*; *Ben Ellan*; *Ben Vooar* (2); and the recently-acquired *Ben Ain*, the youngest (built 1924), a mere 15 years old. As the conflict developed, the island became home to branches of all three armed services, with extensive and heavily-populated training camps. It was also home for many internees and, later, many prisoners-of-war. This large increase in the number of island residents, plus the extra demands of the military, led to traffic requirements far in excess of peacetime demands. The five 'Ben Boats' of the Ramsey Steamship Company became the island's second life-line for the transport of essential supplies, and continued to work intensively under very difficult conditions.

The trading activities of J.B. Kee (1930) Ltd. were reduced when the *Fawn* was lost in March 1940 due to an accident under the railway coal tip in Garston Docks, when she capsized and sank. She was subsequently refloated and sold, leaving the *J.B. Kee* as the sole remaining ship of the 1930 company.

The Ramsey Steamship Company, too, was to lose one ship due to an accident. Under wartime conditions, lights to guide shipping were extinguished for the duration of hostilities, and vessels sailed in complete darkness, a hazard which was to lead to the loss of the *Ben Veg*. At 2.00 a.m. on the 22nd May 1941, the *Ben Veg* was following an easterly course in blackout conditions north of the Point of Ayre, heading for Whitehaven, when she was in collision with an unlit motor ship, the *Brittany*, sailing in a north-bound convoy. The *Brittany's* stem caught the *Ben Veg* on her starboard side and inflicted serious damage. Fortunately, no injuries to crew resulted, and it was decided to attempt to beach the vessel at

Peel. However, by 6.00 a.m. water was entering the engine room at such a rate that the pumps could not cope, and the steamer had to be abandoned. From their lifeboat, the six crew members watched until the *Ben Veg* sank at noon some eight miles off the Point of Ayre. Sea conditions were such that their small lifeboat could not reach the Isle of Man, but the crew were rescued by RAF launch. The sum of £3,500 was subsequently received in compensation for the loss of the *Ben Veg*, the company's first vessel.

Wartime conditions made it impossible to find a replacement ship. Most shipping companies had suffered similar losses, and there was an acute shortage of vessels. Nothing remotely suitable came on the market until conditions began to ease somewhat in 1944. In the meantime, the four remaining ships carried on throughout the war. Inflation had set in, and freight rates had risen. Under these new conditions, the Manager's salary was increased to £8 per week. At the 29th Annual General Meeting in 1942, a dividend of 10% was announced, a level which was maintained in 1943, and exceeded in 1944 when it rose to 25%. In June 1944 the 309-ton steamer *Crossbill* became available, somewhat larger than the company's ships to date, but worthy of interest. A bid of £8,000 secured her, and she sailed from Seaham Harbour to Douglas with coal, before moving to Ramsey for damage repairs. In the following month she was engaged in carrying Admiralty stores for HMS *President*, next a 21-day trip coaling for lighthouses, then victualling for the Royal Navy, before settling into work for the island traffic. Unfortunately, the year 1944 ended badly when in November the *Crossbill* (not yet renamed) collided with a tanker in the River Mersey and was out of commission until the end of December for repairs.

So in 1945, the fleet had been restored to its complement of five, some wartime regulations were relaxed, and once again a dividend of 25% was declared.

The Ramsey company's only total loss during the second World War was the tiny *Ben Veg (1)*, run down and sunk when crossing the Irish Sea in May 1941. *[Douglas Cochrane, World Ship Photo Library]*

Ben Veen (1) in the Mersey. *[Roy Fenton collection]*

The post-war years

A period of austerity followed the cessation of hostilities, as industries attempted to return to their normal peacetime production. There was a general shortage of raw materials, and certain supplies were still rationed. The *Ben Varrey*, now over 30 years old and the smallest ship in the fleet, was ripe for disposal, and in September 1946 was sold for £4,000. In October the *Yarmouth Trader* (like the *Crossbill*, a larger vessel of over 300 tons), came on the market for £7,250. Though only six years younger than the *Ben Varrey*, her capacity was

greater, so purchase was agreed and the vessel underwent survey at Wallsend-on-Tyne in the following month. It was agreed that *Crossbill* should be renamed *Ben Veen* and the *Yarmouth Trader* would become *Ben Jee* (2).

Ben Jee (2) at West Quay, Ramsey. *[Company archives]*

The *J.B. Kee*, still sailing for J.B. Kee (1930) Ltd., earned an unexpected bonus on 2nd July 1948, when, outward-bound from the Mersey, she went to the rescue of the Caernarvon steamer *Elidir* (423/1903), which was drifting with engine-failure near the Lune Buoy. The *J.B. Kee* towed the stricken vessel back into Birkenhead, wisely refusing offers of help from Liverpool tugboats until close to the dockside. A salvage court later awarded a substantial sum to owners and crew for services rendered.

On Ramsey quayside, the proliferation of motor lorries had led to the virtual abandonment of the Harbour Tramway, which in latter years had been used only intermittently. The outward shipments of grain, formerly a regular export, had ceased. Imports of coal for the Isle of Man Railway (and occasionally iron rails from Workington) seem to have been the last items carried over the Tramway, which saw its final coal train in June 1949. (The rails remained *in situ* for a time, in case of need, but were lifted or covered over between 1955 and 1957.)

The five 'Ben Boats' were managed profitably in the post-war period, enabling shareholders to enjoy a regular 25% dividend. *Ben Jee* (2) had a relatively short career with the company. She had run aground near the Point of Ayre on the 22nd November 1952, been refloated and taken first to Ramsey, and then to Birkenhead for dry dock inspection. Evidently, it was considered that repair work would be too expensive for this 32-year old vessel, and she was sold for demolition in February 1953 and broken up at Preston.

A replacement vessel was not secured until March 1954, when the third product of the Manchester Dry Docks Company joined the fleet. Smaller than the two most recent acquisitions, she was the 34-year-old *Beaconia*, purchased from the Wilson Steamship Company of Whitehaven for £3,600 to become *Ben Varrey* (2), sister ship to *Ben Ain* and the lost *Ben Seyr*. Later in the year it was agreed to accept an offer of £3,000 for the *Ben Vooar* (2) to be delivered to the

Ben Jee (2) aground at the Point of Ayre, Isle of Man in December 1952. Despite the apparent lack of damage, she was not repaired and was broken up at Preston. *[W.A. Mackie, Company archives]*

Clyde for demolition in January 1956. The fleet was briefly increased to six with the purchase in December 1955 of the Douglas-registered *Kyle Rhea* for £3,000 from an island owner, Mrs. Ellen Cubbin. This was the last steam-driven ship to be purchased by the company. She was renamed *Ben Maye* in April 1956 and remained in the Douglas registry. At the 42nd Annual General Meeting in 1955, the dividend had fallen from its previous level of 25% to 20%.

These 1954-55 purchases of two 30-year-old steam-powered vessels appeared to be very much an interim measure, for the directors were already actively considering the possibility of adding a motor vessel to the fleet. Coal was no longer the major import it had once been. The conversion of the island's Pulrose Power Station from coal to oil firing, and the replacement of town gas with liquid petroleum gas imported in tankers, plus the general decline in demand for solid fuel, meant that the character of trade was changing. Coal imports had declined by two thirds.

Modernisation and the decline of steam
The commission of a new motor ship and the modernisation of the fleet were considerations in 1956, but the company was unable to find a British shipyard which would guarantee a firm price and delivery date. Consequently, the second-hand market was scoured in the search for a suitable vessel. It transpired that a Norwegian-owned coaster, the nine-year-old 407-ton motor vessel *Tamara*, would become available in July 1956 on the completion of its existing charter. The company offered to buy at £45,000 subject to the repair of collision damage and delivery to a west coast port.

Above: the *Beaconia* was bought from Whitehaven owners in 1954 and renamed *Ben Varrey* (2). *[J. and M. Clarkson]*

Below: *Ben Maye* (1) in a busy corner of Douglas harbour. *[Company archives]*

In the event, an increased offer of £50,000 had to be made to secure the *Tamara*, which entered the Ramsey fleet on the 26th July 1956 as the *Ben Rein* (3). Repairs completed at Bowling, she commenced trading in November 1956, when, at the 43rd Annual General Meeting, a dividend of 20% was announced once again, a level which was to be maintained until 1964. Meanwhile, the rundown of the steamers continued with *Ben Varrey* (2) being sold to breakers in Dublin early in 1957.

Ben Varrey (2) partly demolished at Dublin, 9th June 1957. *[George Osbon, World Ship Photo Library]*

Ben Rein (3), the first motor vessel. *[Ken Cunnington]*

On the 5th November 1957 the last act in the story of J.B. Kee (1930) Ltd. was played out when that firm's remaining steamship *J.B. Kee* was lost in the Mersey Estuary. On passage carrying gravel to Liverpool, the cargo shifted in heavy weather, the vessel developed an alarming list, and her crew of six had to be taken off by the New Brighton Lifeboat. She was not replaced, and the company was wound up.

The ex-Dutch coaster *Ben Vooar* (3). *[J. and M. Clarkson]*

Meanwhile, the directors of the Ramsey Steamship Company, pleased with the operation of their first motor ship, were considering the purchase of a second, and successfully offered £36,000 for the Dutch-built 427-ton *Mudo*, which in July 1959 was renamed *Ben Vooar* (3). The *Ben Vooar* (3) had been built in 1950 for an owner/master, and consequently had more luxurious accommodation for her captain than was usual. Booth W. Kelly Ltd. at Ramsey Shipyard fitted new equipment enabling the engines to be controlled directly from the bridge, thus economising on crew. The purchase of a third motor ship was discussed, and it was agreed to dispose of the ageing *Ben Ellan*, sold to shipbreakers in July 1961 for £2,400.

Ben Ellan (1) leaving Whitehaven. *[Roy Fenton collection]*

Above: Ben Varrey (3) takes to the water at Westerbroek on 10th November 1962, proudly flying a Red Ensign.

Below: trials in March 1963 saw her running under the Dutch flag, still being in builder's hands.
[Company archives]

The fleet now consisted of three steamships, *Ben Ain*, *Ben Maye*, and *Ben Veen*, each about 40-years old (two of which were due for survey in 1962), and motor ships *Ben Rein* (3) and *Ben Vooar* (3), respectively 14 and 11 years old. Audited profits earned by the two motor ships, allowing for depreciation, were £7,678 per ship. It was deemed impractical to convert one of the steamships to a motor vessel, though this was considered. Priority was to be given to the purchase of a third motor ship with a cargo capacity of about 500 tons. By September 1961 contract work for the East Downshire Steamship Company had been obtained, so it became urgently necessary to have another vessel available to cope with the East Downshire Company's trade. It was decided to commission the building of a new vessel, designed to meet the company's specific requirements. Tenders received from the five British yards which showed interest ranged from £94,000 to £140,000, whilst estimates from six Dutch yards varied from £77,000 to £82,000. The directors would have preferred their work to be done by a British yard, but the difference in cost was too great. In addition, the successful experience of the Dutch yards with small motor vessels was deemed to be another weighty factor in reaching a decision. Pleased with the operation of the well-built *Ben Vooar* (3), the directors opted to give the work to the same shipyard, that of E.J. Smit at Westerbroek, at an estimated cost of £81,667, with a delivery date of December 1962, later amended to 1st February 1963. The resulting contract dated November 1961 was the first for a new ship since the original *Ben Veg* of 1914. The name chosen for the new vessel continued the company's tradition. She was to be *Ben Varrey* (3), whose completion would represent a considerable increase in size over the other vessels in the fleet.

In March 1962 the directors learnt of the death of Secretary and Manager James Ramsay. Mr. Ramsay had been with the company since 1928, first as personal assistant to J.B. Kee, taking over from him in 1934 at the age of 32. He had guided the company through some difficult periods, and appreciation was recorded of James Ramsay's loyal, conscientious and energetic service. Appointed in his stead was Mr. Bernard Thomas Swales, who had joined the company straight from school in 1935 and had become Assistant Manager.

The keel of the *Ben Varrey* (3) was laid in June 1962, the launch taking place on the 10th November. The vessel was delivered at Delfzijl after trials on the 14th March 1963. Her completion had been delayed by about six weeks due to the severe winter. The total cost, including radar and radio equipment, had amounted to £86,209. Her arrival in the Isle of Man was accompanied by a special celebration, and the directors held a meeting on board in Douglas harbour, their first meeting afloat and outside Ramsey.

Meantime, the steamship *Ben Veen* had been sold for £1,800 in December 1962 for demolition in Ireland, and the *Ben Ain* (1) followed (for £1,600) in June 1963.

On the 8th July 1963 the motor ship *Ben Rein* (3) collided in dense fog off the Point of Ayre with the *Wyre Revenge* and suffered severe bow damage, which necessitated dry dock repair work and a special survey. Whilst the ship was out of commission, the Isle of Man Coal Importers' Association, perhaps sensing another change, chose the opportunity to be highly critical of the company's policy of replacing 200-ton steamers with 400-ton motor ships. The Association alleged that merchants who took less than a complete cargo suffered 'unwonted costs and inconvenience,' and went on to claim that the company dictated when, where, and how much a merchant might receive, and to which port it would be carried. The Association requested that the small vessel (i.e. the *Ben Maye*, the last surviving steamship) be retained or replaced with a vessel of similar capacity; that two-port discharges should be offered; and that, if necessary, the company's ships should carry less than the optimum quantity.

A patient and measured reply was drafted for the Association, pointing out that arrangements for part cargoes and deliveries to more than one port were already available. The response went on to explain the difficulties of small tonnage. The post-war years had seen a change in the type and size of ship engaged in the coastal trade. The steamships carried small cargoes in relation to their size, since so much space was needed for engine, boilers and bunkers. Replacing the steamships with motor vessels of similar dimensions offered much greater cargo-carrying capacity, and very small ships were not suitable for the Irish Sea in winter conditions. Thus the trend had been to acquire fewer but larger units to carry the same amount of freight. The Association was reminded that six small coasting companies trading in the Irish Sea had gone out of business in recent years, and that the Ramsey Steamship Company was facing economic facts in trying to survive.

After the disposal of two of the three steamships earlier in the year, the fleet at the end of 1963 consisted of four vessels: the three motor ships, *Ben Varrey* (3), *Ben Vooar* (3), and *Ben Rein* (3), and the steamship *Ben Maye*. In December 1963 came the 50th Annual General Meeting of the company, at which a dividend of 20% was declared. The replacement of *Ben Maye*, which, it was believed, was unlikely to remain in service for more than 14 months, was debated early in 1964. After reviewing the current prices for second-hand ships, the directors agreed that a new vessel was preferable. Tenders ranging between £75,000 and £92,000 were subsequently received, the delivery time being from 10 to 16 months. The order for the new ship, to be named *Ben Veg* (2) was placed with Cleland's of Wallsend-on-Tyne, at an estimated cost of £77,400.

Ben Veg (2), built for the company on the Tyne. [J. and M. Clarkson]

It was during 1964 that the company gained a somewhat strange contract. The 'pirate radio' ship, 'Radio Caroline' was operating beyond the three-mile limit off Ramsey Bay, and the company was invited to act as agents. The Manx Government had no objection, and the company took up the contract to deliver supplies of fuel, fresh water, and general stores as required for a fee of £42 per week. (The company continued to act as agents for the radio ship until March 1967.)

At the close of 1964, the *Ben Maye*, last of the company's steamships, was sold for £3,750 (less 2.5% brokerage) for breaking-up at Troon, and at the 51st Annual General Meeting a dividend of 20% was declared once again.

The new *Ben Veg* (2) was completed on the Tyne on the 3rd March 1965. The final cost was £82,506. She loaded fertilisers at Middlesbrough on the 9th March, and arrived at Ramsey on the 13th to discharge part-cargo, the rest being for Douglas. The directors invited guests to inspect the new vessel. At 346-tons, the *Ben Veg* (2) temporarily reversed the trend towards larger vessels, as she was somewhat smaller than the other motor ships in the fleet, but deliberately so, as she had been designed to limits imposed by the harbours at Laxey and Castletown. At that time, the vessels still carried regular shipments of grain to Laxey for Corlett's flour mills.

It was during 1965 that negotiations began for the Ramsey Steamship Company to take over the business of Leonard Callow, last manager of the Douglas Shipping Company, and since 1933 principal ship broker and sub-agent for Lloyd's in Douglas. The firm had been converted to a limited company, L.M. Callow Ltd., in 1957, when Gifford Rowe (who had joined the office staff in 1942) and Mrs. Isobel Callow joined Leonard Callow as directors. By 1965 Leonard Callow had decided to retire, but Gifford Rowe wished to continue. The Ramsey directors agreed to acquire the business, and to offer Gifford Rowe the post of Assistant Manager, in which capacity he could look after former Callow clients. Thus it was that the Ramsey Steamship Company purchased the goodwill and shares with a view to taking over the Douglas-based firm on the 1st January 1966. The company thenceforth maintained offices in both Ramsey and Douglas, a practice which subsequently proved uneconomic.

It was becoming increasingly difficult to recruit labour to unload ships, a problem which was partially overcome by the purchase of a self-propelled mobile crane, which could be driven by road to ports on the island as required. The acquisition of this crane reduced considerably the turn-round time for ships in port, and proved to be a wise investment. Unfortunately, later in 1966 the company's four ships had a period of some seven weeks' enforced idleness due to the seamen's strike. However, even in this difficult period, the company operated some 'mercy runs' to bring in essential supplies. The earnings of these voyages were donated to the King George's Fund for Sailors. Problems ashore also led the company to consider the introduction of container traffic.

As the 1960s drew to a close, the problem of ship replacement had to be considered again. Current costs for new ships seemed prohibitive, and decisions were deferred. Dividends continued to be paid at 25%, and at the end of the decade manager Bernard Swales was invited to join the Board. The 407-ton *Ben Rein* (3), the company's first motor vessel, built 1947 and purchased second-hand in 1956, was approaching 25 years of age, and was due for special survey in 1972. It seemed clear that the future policy should be to replace the current fleet with larger vessels. Consequently, when the General Steam Navigation Company placed their vessel *Plover* on the market, she was inspected at Newport Docks in October 1971 and an offer of £60,000 was submitted, with the possibility of increasing the bid to £65,000 if necessary. In the event, however, a third offer of £67,000, subject to dry dock examination, was necessary to secure the deal, and arrangements were made to take over the ship on the 19th November 1971.

Just after midnight on the 13th October 1971 a bomb exploded aboard the *Ben Vooar* (3) moored in Cork Harbour. Presumably, the intention was to sink the vessel. In the event, the ship remained afloat, but was out of service for eleven days whilst repairs costing some £3,000 were carried out. Subsequently, County Cork paid £1,700 towards the cost of this work.

On arrival in Ramsey in November 1971, the newly-acquired *Plover* was renamed *Ben Veen* (2), and the *Ben Rein* (3) was offered for sale. The Ramsey Steamship Company's business was now increasingly centred on Douglas, and it was decided to close the Ramsey office and purchase a property and transfer operations to North Quay, Douglas.

The *Ben Vooar's* unfortunate experience in Cork Harbour proved to be a forerunner of a disaster of a different kind in the north of Ireland. Approaching Portrush in ballast on 3rd June 1975, she ran aground near Inishowen Head and suffered bottom damage. She was assisted by two fishing vessels and taken in tow to be beached near Greencastle, County Donegal. On the 12th June she was moved, as the company minutes record, to dry dock in Londonderry, where she was inspected as a result of 'contact' with Inishowen Head. In view of the vessel's age, it was deemed uneconomic to spend upwards of £70,000 on repairs, so she was offered for sale 'as is, where is' at Londonderry. A buyer was found in August, and she was subsequently repaired to sail again as the *Arran Firth*. The *Ben Vooar* (3) was not immediately replaced, as it was reported that cargoes were hard to find in summer, but in the following year the company acquired their largest ship yet. The 500-ton *Gretchen Weston*, built 1966, was available at the yard of James Lamont, Greenock. She was bought in January 1976, re-registered at Ramsey, and entered the fleet as *Ben Ain* (2), making her first voyage under new ownership on the 19th January carrying a cargo of cement from Runcorn to Douglas.

Problems of the 1970s and early 1980s

The 1970s proved a worrying time for the company. The 346-ton *Ben Veg* (2), built new for the company in 1965, was now the smallest ship in the fleet. The increasing number of pleasure craft crowding Laxey harbour had led to that port being closed to commercial shipping in 1973, and the need for a small vessel to enter its confines had therefore disappeared. Cargoes of grain for the Laxey Mills were thenceforth shipped to Ramsey and carried the intervening ten miles in motor lorries. Prolonged troubles in the coal-mining industry robbed the company of much of its regular trade, and even when the strikes were settled, shipments of coal did not return to their previous levels. The Ramsey Steamship Company had perforce to enter upon a period of retrenchment and damage limitation. The *Ben Veg* (2), after being laid up at Ramsey for a period, and due for special survey, was offered for sale in 1978 and purchased by the Tyne Ship Repair Group at South Shields. Since her arrival in 1965, the *Ben Veg* (2) had made 930 voyages for the company, and carried 355,000 metric tonnes of cargo. With her departure, the fleet was reduced to three, *Ben Varrey* (3) built 1963, *Ben Veen* (2) built 1965, and the latest and largest acquisition *Ben Ain* (2) built 1966. Even larger tonnage was considered, but the coastal trade was still passing through what was said to be 'a lean time,' with added difficulties caused by inflation, so no further action was taken.

The depression continued into the 1980s. Manager Bernard Swales retired in 1983, after a total of 48 years with the company. He had proved a loyal and conscientious servant, seeing the company through good times and bad. He was now succeeded by Gifford Rowe. A proposed merger/take-over was rejected. This was at least the third occasion when rivals had been beaten off when bidding for the company. In May 1984 the *Ben Veen* (2) was laid up and offered for sale, a buyer not being found until December. Further industrial unrest on the mainland and the strike of the National Union of Seamen adversely affected the company's activities. Trading continued with only two ships in the hopes of an early end to problems and an upturn in trade. Hopes were dashed, however. The *Ben Varrey* (3), having been towed into Ramsey with severe engine trouble in December 1984, was promptly laid up and offered for sale, going for scrap in August 1985. In this dismal period, only the *Ben Ain* (2) remained in service.

Recovery, 1988-2000

More optimistic forecasts of the trading situation led to the consideration of replacement tonnage in 1987. In April 1988 the 499-ton *Bulk Moon* was inspected at Grangemouth and purchased, entering the Ramsey fleet in August 1988 as *Ben Vane*. Eighteen months later, the even-larger *River Tamar* was acquired in November 1990 to be renamed *Ben Ellan* (2), bringing the fleet total temporarily back to three, for it was hoped to sell *Ben Ain* (2). At this period, Mr. Anthony

Ben Vooar (3) in dry dock at Londonderry after her grounding in June 1975. *[John Doherty, Company archives]*

Gordon Kennish was appointed Manager and Secretary on the retirement of Gifford Rowe.

A period of prosperity was beckoning, and in April 1995, when the company learnt that the motor vessel *Vendome* (ex-*Peroto*) had been seized at Plymouth and was being offered for sale by Lloyd's Bank, representatives were sent to investigate. Negotiations for purchase were approved, but, as in previous bargaining, the company was obliged to make an increased offer to secure the vessel, before she joined the fleet as *Ben Maye* (2).

The organisation and smooth running of a small shipping company is never without its problems, many of which cannot be predicted. Difficulties are particularly acute when a vessel is out of commission for some unforeseen reason, and cargoes must be diverted or lost. The *Ben Vane* was unfortunately out of action for six weeks after being towed from Workington with a gearbox problem. In June 1997 the *Ben Ellan* (2) came in contact with the North Arklow Buoy and suffered damage to propeller and tailshaft. A costly tow to dry dock in Liverpool, repairs amounting to some £50,000, and the vessel out of service for three weeks, did not help matters. Shortly afterwards, the *Ben Maye* (2) lost a month's sailings due to a severely worn crankshaft.

Since 1998 the company has maintained its own shore engineers based at East Quay, Ramsey. Here, marine engineering work is undertaken both for the company and also for other owners of fishing vessels, coasters, etc. A wide range of outside work is also undertaken, including the fabrication and repair of agricultural machinery.

Recorded in the company minute book for April 1998 is the news that divers working some twenty miles off Douglas had discovered the wreck of *Ben Rein* (1), sunk seventy years earlier in 1918. The divers sought permission to remove certain items, such as the ship's bell. Permission was granted, but nothing further was heard from the applicants.

Ben Ellan (2) was put up for sale in April 1998, but no firm offers were received immediately. In the same month, *Ben Vane* returned to service after tailshaft repairs and docking surveys. By mid-1999 the company was actively seeking a fourth ship to join the fleet. The 997-ton *Triumph*, built in 1986 and owned by Becks of Groningen, became available for inspection at Goole. A purchase price was agreed, and delivery, after dry docking, was arranged for October 1999. She was to be *Ben Varrey* (4). Meantime, *Ben Vane* suffered a recurrence of gearbox problems, exacerbated by a delay in the delivery of spare parts, and an engine special survey was undertaken in March 2000. In the year 2000, the latest acquisition *Ben Varrey* (4) was trading on the open/spot market but finding good freight rates and cargoes hard to come by.

In March 2001 the *Ben Ellan* (2) successfully delivered a cargo of logs from Campbeltown to Annan, in Dumfries and Galloway, the first time for some thirty years that a commercial vessel had entered this small port. In July 2001 the company agreed to sell *Ben Vane* to a Scottish company, who renamed her *Ben Nevis*. The fleet has thus returned to a total of three: *Ben Ellan*, *Ben Maye*, and *Ben Varrey*

The future
The Ramsey Steamship Company has traded successfully for 90 years. It is a genuinely independent undertaking and remains largely a 'family' enterprise, in that many of the shares of the founders have been handed down from generation to generation, and rarely come on the market. In its 90 years of its existence, the company has had only five Managers:

John Brown Kee	1913-1934
James Ramsay	1934-1962
Bernard T. Swales	1962-1983
Gifford T. Rowe	1983-1991
Anthony G. Kennish	1991-

Over the years, the directors have successfully resisted mergers and take-over bids, and have survived in business when many of the would-be owners have failed. They have adjusted efficiently to different conditions and changing times, and remain financially sound, profits being ploughed back into the business. The company has always bought new tonnage out of money generated by its own cash-flow, and has no debts. Competition has likewise been defeated, and the company thrives today by concentrating on what it does best - that is, the carriage of single bulk cargoes for individual traders, leaving the part-loads and mixed cargoes for others to ship. The company also offers stevedoring services and expertise in dealing with freight as diverse as coal, stone, heavy lift and project cargoes. An important part of the business is acting as shipping agents for cruise ships, tenders, tankers, general cargo and offshore supply vessels. The Lloyd's agency work remains the responsibility of the Managing Director.

Ben Ellan (2) leaves St. Sampsons, 16th May 2001. *[Peter Stewart]*

The present Board of Directors can boast family links with the founders. It consists of Dr. John Crennell Kee (grandson of founder John Thomas Kee and son of the first Manager, John Brown Kee, and who completed 26 years as company chairman in 2002); Captain Ramsey Kee Cringle (the new Chairman, son of Dorothy Campbell Cringle, nee Kee, and grandson of John Brown Kee); Gifford T. Rowe (former Manager); and Anthony G. Kennish (present Manager). Captain Ramsey Cringle followed a seafaring career, and for some years was master of one of the company's ships. The whole enterprise is administered by a shore staff of only four: Anthony G. Kennish (Manager and Company Secretary), Chris van Buul (Marine Superintendent), Mark Bumfrey (agency), and Miss Muriel Cain (accounts).

The Ramsey Steamship Company enjoys a high reputation, not only in the Isle of Man, where the 'Ben' boats are regarded with affection, but throughout the coastal trade. The company has launched the careers of many Manx seafarers, some of whom moved on to positions of responsibility in larger undertakings. Not a few ship's masters, including some for the Isle of Man Steam Packet Company, began their working life on a Ramsey 'Ben' boat.

In 1993 the company was honoured by the Isle of Man Post Office when a definitive stamp issue carried a representation of *Ben Veg* (2) leaving Ramsey harbour.

Derivation of Ramsey Steamship Company names

In the Isle of Man, the Ramsey Steamship Company vessels have always been known as the 'Ben Boats,' an inevitable consequence of the Company's traditional naming policy. In Manx Gaelic, the word 'Ben' means 'girl' or 'woman.' A translation of the various names is as follows.

BEN AIN	Our lady.
BEN BLANCHE	Hybrid Manx/English from the original name of the ship, *Sarah Blanche*.
BEN ELLAN	Lady of the isle.
BEN JEE	Goddess.
BEN MAY	Derived from the original name *Glen May*.
BEN MAYE	Lady Maye/yellow lady.
BEN REIN	Queen.
BEN SEYR	Gentle lady.
BEN VANE	White lady.
BEN VARREY	Girl of the sea or mermaid
BEN VEEN	Darling girl.
BEN VEG	Little woman or wife.
BEN VOOAR	Big lady.

Colour scheme

Funnel:	Black with red band bearing a white Maltese cross.
Houseflag:	Blue, with a white Maltese cross and letters 'R S S Co.' (see back cover for illustrations)
Steamers' hulls:	Black with red boot topping.
Motor ships' hulls:	Grey with green or black boot topping.
Masts:	Buff ('mast colour').
Inside bulwarks:	Buff ('mast colour').
Steamers' casings:	Brown.
Motorships' casings:	White.

The Ramsey Steamship Company's latest acquisition, *Ben Varrey* (4), at Ramsey on 28th October 1999. *[Roy Crisp]*

Above: *Ben Veg* (1) in Preston Dock. *[J. and M. Clarkson]*

Below: *Ben Rein* (1). *[T.H. Midwood, courtesy John Cowley]*

RAMSEY STEAMSHIP CO. LTD. FLEET LIST

Ben Varrey (1) . *[J. and M. Clarkson]*

1. BEN VEG (1) 1914-1941

O.N.87583 159g 61n 95.0 x 19.1 x 8.5 feet.
C. 2-cyl. by Gauldie, Gillespie and Co., Glasgow; 50 NHP, 200 IHP, 9½ knots.
8.1914: Completed by the Larne Shipbuilding Co., Larne (Yard No. 65).
19.8.1914: Registered in the ownership of the Ramsey Steamship Co. Ltd., Ramsey as BEN VEG.
22.5.1941: Sank eight miles north of the Point of Ayre following a collision with the motor vessel BRITTANY which took place six miles west of the Mull of Galloway whilst on a voyage from Carnlough to Whitehaven in ballast.
25.11.1941: Register closed.

2. BEN REIN (1) 1916-1918

O.N.121247 212g 79n 110.0 x 22.1 x 8.3 feet.
C. 2-cyl. by Colin Houston and Co., Glasgow; 40 NHP, 275 IHP, 9½ knots.
26.6.1905: Launched by George Brown and Co., Greenock (Yard No. 28).
7.1905: Completed.
13.7.1905: Registered in the ownership of Steel and Bennie Ltd., Glasgow as STARLING.
2.11.1915: Sold to William E. Fisher, Maryport.
2.8.1916: Acquired by the Ramsey Steamship Co. Ltd., Ramsey.
17.10.1916: Renamed BEN REIN.
7.2.1918: Sunk by gunfire from the German submarine UB 57 in position 35 miles west north west of Liverpool Bar whilst on a voyage from Liverpool to Belfast with general cargo. Her crew of seven was rescued by the steamer NORMAN and landed at Whitehaven the next day.
9.2.1918: Register closed.

3. WHITESTONE/BEN VARREY (1) 1917-1946

O.N.136334 198g 71n 100.3 x 20.1 x 8.8 feet.
C. 2-cyl. by A. Jeffrey and Co. Ltd., Alloa; 32 NHP, 230 IHP, 8 knots.
1948: Alpha oil engine 3-cyl. 2SCSA by A/S Frederikshavns Jernstoberi and Maskinfabrik, Frederikshavn; 174 BHP, 8 knots.
1914: Completed by Archibald Jeffrey and Co. Ltd., Alloa (Yard No. 11).
13.11.1914: Registered in the ownership of Archibald R. Robertson (32/64) and Robert Robertson (32/64) (John M. Paton, manager), Glasgow as WHITESTONE.
6.6.1917: Acquired by the Ramsey Steamship Co. Ltd., Ramsey.
12.9.1919: Renamed BEN VARREY.
12.9.1946: Sold to the Williamstown Shipping Co. Ltd. (Comben, Longstaffe and Co. Ltd., managers), London for £4,000.
7.10.1946: Renamed GLOUCESTERBROOK.
3.1947: Sold to Partrederiet 'Herluf Trolle' (H.R. Madsen and K.E. Madsen, managers), Naestved, Denmark and renamed LISE EG.
1947: Manager became J.E. Madsen.
1948: Fitted with oil engine.
1954: Sold to I/S 'Johan' (Hans Hermansen, manager), Marstal, Denmark and renamed JOHAN.
1969: Manager became Jorn Rasmussen.
1970: Sold to Albert K. Madsen Partrederi, Marstal.
1972: Owners became I/S Albert K. Madsen, Marstal.
1972: Renamed SEA EXPLORER II.
1973: Sold to Skipdahl Ltd., Nassau, Bahamas.
6.4.1977: Arrived at Monkeberg on the Kiel Fjord in tow of the tug LORBAS from Egernsund for breaking up by Zerssen and Co.

Above: Ben Vooar (1). [T.H. Midwood, courtesy John Cowley]   *Below: Ben Rein (2) . [T.H. Midwood, Company archives]*

4. REDSTONE/BEN VOOAR (2) 1918-1919

O.N.137825 227g 90n 112.1 x 20.1 x 8.8 feet.
C. 2-cyl. by A. Jeffrey and Co., Alloa; 8 knots.
10.1916: Completed by A. Jeffrey and Co., Alloa (Yard No. 16).
12.10.1916: Registered in the ownership of Archibald Robertson and Robert Robertson, Glasgow as REDSTONE.
12.12.1916: Sold to Charles G. Ewing, Birkenhead.
27.9.1917: Sold to Charles A. Ewing, Chester (William J. Ireland, Liverpool, manager).
21.10.1918: Acquired by the Ramsey Steamship Co. Ltd., Ramsey.
1919: Renamed BEN VOOAR.
21.6.1936: Wrecked 15 yards off the seaward end of the West Pier, Castlerock at the entrance to the River Bann whilst on a voyage from Birkenhead to Coleraine with a cargo of coal. The crew of six was rescued by the pilot boat.

5. BEN REIN (2) 1919-1921

O.N.120783 156g 61n 105.0 x 21.1 x 7.1 feet.
C. 2-cyl. by Fisher and Co., Paisley.
8.5.1905: Launched by John Fullerton and Co., Paisley (Yard No. 187).
6.1905: Completed.
10.6.1905: Registered in the ownership of R. and W. Paul, Ipswich as TERN.
6.4.1912: Sold to Sir Richard H.W. Bulkeley (William O. Griffiths, manager), Beaumaris.
6.6.1919: Acquired by the Ramsey Steamship Co. Ltd., Ramsey.
17.9.1919: Renamed BEN REIN.
29.10.1921: Sold to John George, Trevine, Pembroke.
24.12.1936: Sold to the Ilfracombe Coal and Salvage Co. Ltd. (George H. Chenhalls, manager), Ilfracombe.
27.9.1939: Sold to the Straits Steamship Co. Ltd. (Lovell D. Mack, manager), Liverpool.
29.2.1940: Sold to the Southern Salvage Co. Ltd. (Awdry V. Cole, manager), Southampton.

Ben Seyr at Preston with the white plate carrying the Maltese cross missing from her funnel. *[World Ship Photo Library]*

17.2.1941: Mined and sunk about three and a half miles east of the Manacles whilst on a voyage from Plymouth to Falmouth in ballast. Two of her crew of seven were lost.
11.3.1941: Register closed.

6. BEN SEYR 1920-1938

O.N. 87585 274g 103n 120.0 x 22.1 x 9.0 feet.
C. 2-cyl. by Manchester Dry Docks Co. Ltd., Ellesmere Port; 41 NHP, 275 IHP, 10 knots.
11.10.1919: Launched by the Manchester Dry Docks Co. Ltd., Ellesmere Port (Yard No.71) for their own account, as DEVESON. She had been laid down for the Shipping Controller as WAR DEVERON, but the order was cancelled in November 1918.
4.1920: Completed.
25.5.1920: Registered in the ownership of the Ramsey Steamship Co. Ltd., Ramsey as BEN SEYR.
2.10.1938: Left Ramsey for Cardiff with a cargo of oats. After sheltering in Rosslare Bay 5.10.1938 she disappeared, the body of her mate being later washed up on Middleton Sands, between Heysham and Sunderland Point.

7. BEN BLANCHE 1923-1933 Iron

O.N.95756 255g 99n 130.0 x 21.1 x 9.7 feet.
C. 2-cyl. by Ross and Duncan, Govan; 55 NHP, 350 IHP, 11 knots.
12.8.1891: Launched by John Fullerton and Co., Paisley (Yard No. 99).
19.9.1891: Registered in the ownership of Joseph Sharp and William A. Waid, Douglas as SARAH BLANCHE.
14.2.1901: Sold to Andrew Knowles and Sons Ltd., Manchester (Herbert Thornley, Douglas, manager).
23.8.1921: Owner became Andrew Knowles Wharves Ltd., Manchester (Herbert Thornley, Douglas, manager).
20.2.1923: Acquired by the Ramsey Steamship Co. Ltd., Ramsey.
30.7.1923: Renamed BEN BLANCHE.
17.12.1933: Wrecked in fog at Oxwich Point, near Mumbles, South Wales whilst on a voyage from Dunoon to Swansea with a cargo of potatoes. The crew was rescued by the Mumbles Lifeboat.

8. BEN JEE (1) 1924-1933

O.N. 143355 341g 175n 119.41 x 23.81 x 10.41 feet.
T. 3-cyl. by N.V. van de Kuy & van de Ree, Rotterdam.
1919: Completed by N.V. van de Kuy & van de Ree, Rotterdam for Walford Lines Ltd. (George Walford, manager), London as JOLLY BASIL.
1920: Managers became Leopold Walford (London) Ltd.
1924: Acquired by the Ramsey Steamship Co. Ltd., Ramsey and renamed BEN JEE.
1933: Sold to the United Molasses Co. Ltd., London and renamed ATHELRILL.
1940: Owners became the Athel Line Ltd., London.
1948: Sold to the Pure Cane Molasses Co. (British West Indies) Ltd., Georgetown, Demerara; renamed MOLARILL and fitted with tanks in hold to carry petroleum in bulk.
1950: Sold to Charlestown Saw Mills Ltd., Georgetown.
1952: Converted to dry cargo vessel.
1958: Broken up in Georgetown.

9. BEN MAY 1928-1937

O.N.102899 154g 63n 101.6 x 17.5 x 9.3 feet.
C. 2-cyl. by Kincaid and Co. Ltd., Greenock; 9 knots.
8.1894: Completed by T.B. Seath and Co., Glasgow (Yard No. 292).
24.8.1894: Registered in the ownership of Thomas B. Briggs, Sunderland as READY.
29.3.1895: Sold to Charles H. Pile, London.
8.1895: Sold to Perroud et Compagnie, Nantes, France and renamed MARCHE DROIT.
1898: Sold to Y. Lefiblec et Compagnie, Lannion, France.
2.1.1902: Registered in the ownership of Edwin Qualtrough, Peel, Isle of Man as READY.
18.1.1902: Renamed GLENMAY.
5.2.1902: Sold to Steamship 'Glenmay' Ltd. (Henry Quayle, manager), Peel.
10.12.1902: Manager became Edwin Qualtrough.
4.2.1914: Sold to William Darlington, Garston.
8.8.1921: Sold to Alfred H. Connell, Liverpool.
20.9.1921: Sold to the Solway Shipping Co. Ltd. (James B. Care, manager), Whitehaven.
1.11.1923: Manager became Alfred H. Connell.
16.6.1926: Sold to Edwin I. Murphy, Waterford.
20.2.1928: Acquired by the Ramsey Steamship Co. Ltd., Ramsey.
17.10.1928: Renamed BEN MAY.
9.8.1937: Sold to Samuel Gray, Belfast.
14.9.1938: Sold to William Trohear, Dundrum.
14.11.1938: Sprang a leak in the North Channel and foundered in East Tarbert Bay, off the Mull of Galloway, whilst on a voyage from Workington to Dundrum with a cargo of coal. Her crew of four got away in the ship's boat.
24.6.1939: Register closed.

Ben Blanche. [Douglas Cochrane, World Ship Photo Library]

Above: *Ben Jee* (1). *[J. and M. Clarkson]*

Below: *Ben May [Douglas Cochrane, World Ship Photo Library]*

10. BEN ELLAN (1) 1936-1961

O.N.144851 270g 99n 117.1 x 22.2 x 9.1 feet.
C. 2-cyl. by Shields Engineering Co. Ltd., North Shields.
11.1921: Completed by R.B. Harrison and Sons Ltd., Newcastle-upon-Tyne (Yard No.2) for the Wear Steam Shipping Co. Ltd (Thomas Rose, manager), Sunderland as MOORSIDE.
1926: Sold to Robert Rix and Sons, Hull and renamed PEGRIX.
1936: Acquired by the Ramsey Steamship Co. Ltd., Ramsey and renamed BEN ELLAN.
7.1961: Sold to the Hammond Lane Metal Co. Ltd., Dublin for breaking up.
8.7.1961: Work commenced.

Ben Ellan (1), the lower view at Glasgow on 15th July 1960. *[R.J. Scott and J. and M Clarkson collection]*

11. BEN VOOAR (2) 1938-1956

O.N. 136358 274g 99n 120.8 x 22.1 x 9.1 feet.
C. 2-cyl. by A. Jeffrey and Co. Ltd., Alloa.
12.1916: Completed by A. Jeffrey and Co. Ltd., Alloa (Yard No. 15) for Howden Brothers (W.J.R. Harbinson, manager), Larne as CARGAN.
1921: Sold to John Christopher, Waterford.
1926: Sold to K. Williams and Co. Ltd. (John Christopher, manager), Waterford.
1936: Sold to the Larne Steamship Co. Ltd., Larne Harbour.
7.1938: Acquired by the Ramsey Steamship Co. Ltd., Ramsey.
1939: Renamed BEN VOOAR.
18.1.1956: Sold to British Iron and Steel Corporation Ltd.
24.2.1956: Arrived at Port Glasgow for breaking up by Smith and Houston Ltd.

Ben Vooar (2) at Douglas, 31st August 1955. *[F.W. Hawks]*

12. BEN AIN (1) 1938-1963
O.N. 147251 266g 99n 120.0 x 22.1 x 9.1 feet.
C.2-cyl. by Manchester Dry Docks Co. Ltd., Ellesmere Port.
5.3.1924: Launched by Manchester Dry Docks Co. Ltd., Ellesmere Port (Yard No. 73). She had been laid down for the builder's account in 1919.
4.1924: Completed for Thomas Brothers Shipping Co. Ltd., Liverpool as DORIS THOMAS.
1930: Owners became Thomas Coasters Ltd., Liverpool.
1936: Sold to A.F. Henry and MacGregor Ltd., Leith and

renamed DENNIS HEAD.
12.1938: Acquired by the Ramsey Steamship Co. Ltd., Ramsey.
2.1939: Renamed BEN AIN.
5.6.1963: Arrived at Passage West, Cork for demolition by Haulbowline Industries Ltd.

Ben Ain (1) at West Quay, Ramsey 5th August 1962; note the open wheelhouse. *[Edward Gray]*

13. CROSSBILL/BEN VEEN (1) 1944-1962

O.N. 140103 309g 127n 130.0 x 23.2 x 9.5 feet.
C.2-cyl. by Crabtree and Co. Ltd., Great Yarmouth.
12.1920: Completed by Crabtree and Co. Ltd., Great Yarmouth (Yard No. 179) for R. and W. Paul Ltd., Ipswich as CROSSBILL.
1944: Acquired by the Ramsey Steamship Co. Ltd., Ramsey.
1947: Renamed BEN VEEN.
12.1962: Sold to Haulbowline Industries Ltd. for demolition at Passage West, Cork
1.2.1963: Work commenced.

14. BEN JEE (2) 1947-1953

O.N. 143512 312g 125n 130.0 x 23.2 x 9.5 feet.
C. 2-cyl. by Crabtree and Co. Ltd., Great Yarmouth; 45 NHP, 360 IHP, 9 knots.
7.1920: Completed by Crabtree and Co. Ltd., Great Yarmouth (Yard No. 178).
19.7.1920: Registered in the ownership of the Elveden Shipping Co. Ltd. (Griffin Brothers, managers), Cardiff as STERTPOINT.
31.5.1921: Sold to Arthur W. Page (David L. MacIntosh,

Top and bottom: Ben Veen (1). [J.K. Byass; and World Ship Photo Library]

manager), Bristol.
29.12.1926: Sold to Isaac W. Laing, Sunderland.
10.3.1927: Renamed ASHDENE.
17.12.1928: Sold to Frederic W. Gibson, Sunderland.
20.1.1930: Sold to T. Small and Co. (Great Yarmouth) Ltd., Great Yarmouth.
8.2.1930: Renamed YARMOUTH TRADER.
17.12.1931: Sold to the Great Yarmouth Shipping Co. Ltd., Great Yarmouth.
21.10.1946: Acquired by the Ramsey Steamship Co. Ltd., Ramsey.
14.1.1947: Renamed BEN JEE.
20.11.1952: Stranded half a mile south of the Point of Ayre, Isle of Man whilst on a voyage from Carrickfergus to Garston in ballast.
16.12.1952: Refloated and taken to Ramsey Harbour.
2.1.1953: Arrived at Birkenhead to await dry docking. Later sold to British Iron and Steel Corporation Ltd.
19.2.1953: Arrived at Preston for breaking up by T.W. Ward Ltd.
27.6.1953: Register closed.

15. BEN VARREY (2) 1954-1957
O.N. 147211 266g 99n 120.0 x 22.1 x 9.1 feet.
C. 2-cyl. by Manchester Dry Docks Co. Ltd., Manchester; 9 knots.
19.5.1920: Launched by the Manchester Dry Docks Co. Ltd., Ellesmere Port (Yard No. 72) as LOSSIE. She had been laid down for the Shipping Controller as WAR LOSSIE, but cancelled in November 1918.
5.1923: Completed for A. M. Ralli and Son, Liverpool as MIA.
1930: Owners became the Mia Steamship Co. Ltd. (Antonio M. Ralli and Son, managers), Liverpool.

Ben Jee (2), July 1951. [J. and M. Clarkson]

1932: Sold to William F. Cook, Aberdeen.
1937: Sold to the Wilson Steamship Co. Ltd. (T.W. Dixon, manager), Whitehaven and renamed BEACONIA.
1954: Acquired by the Ramsey Steamship Co. Ltd., Ramsey and renamed BEN VARREY.
24.3.1957: Arrived at Dublin for breaking up by the Hammond Lane Foundry Ltd.

Ben Varrey (2) at Douglas. *[Company archives]*

16. BEN MAYE (1) 1955-1964

O.N. 145556 323g 123n 130.2 x 22.6 x 9.6 feet.
C. 2-cyl. by J. Cran and Somerville Ltd., Leith.
22.6.1921: Launched by J. Cran and Somerville Ltd., Leith (Yard No. 127).
1921: Completed for A.F. Henry and MacGregor Ltd., Leith as TOD HEAD.
25.12.1929: Stranded at Peterhead whilst on a voyage from Inverness to Great Yarmouth with a cargo of staves. Her crew was rescued.
16.1.1930: Refloated.
3.3.1930: Arrived at Leith in tow of tug BULLGER and sold to the Grangemouth Dockyard Co. Ltd., Grangemouth, who repaired her.

1930: Sold to Robert Cameron and Co., Glasgow.
1935: Renamed KYLE RHEA.
1940: Sold to Mrs. E.M.M.G. Cubbin (R.A. Colby Cubbin, manager), Douglas.
1955: Acquired by the Ramsey Steamship Co. Ltd., Ramsey and renamed BEN MAYE.
15.12.1964: Arrived at Troon for breaking up after being sold to the British Iron and Steel Corporation Ltd. and allocated to the West of Scotland Shipbreaking Co. Ltd.

17. BEN REIN (3) 1956-1972
O.N. 144865 407g 198n 148.9 x 25.8 x 10.2 feet.
Brons oil engine 7-cyl. 4SCSA by N.V. Appingedammer Bronsmotorenfabriek, Appingedam; 400 BHP, 10 knots.
31.7.1947: Launched by Scheepswerf Delfzijl v/h Sander, Delfzijl (Yard No. 179).
11.1947: Completed for M. Clausen, Haugesund, Norway as LITA.
1950: Owner became D/S A/S Magnhild (M. Clausen, manager), Haugesund.
1954: Sold to Falkum-Hansen Shipping Co. Skibs A/S Arild and Morola A/S (Falkum-Hansen Shipping Co., managers), Oslo, Norway and renamed TAMARA.
26.7.1956: Acquired by the Ramsey Steamship Co. Ltd., Ramsey.
28.7.1956: Renamed BEN REIN.
3.2.1972: Sold to Dimitrios Palmas (Ditrios P. Kalkassinas, manager), Piraeus, Greece and renamed GIANNA P.
1973: Sold to the Capricorn Co. Ltd., Panama.
1976: Sold to Megaloeconomou Brothers, Piraeus, Greece and renamed KAPONAS TH.
1979: Renamed AGIA MONI.
1980: Sold to Capricorn Compania Maritime S.A., Panama City, Panama and renamed GIANNA P.
3.2003: Still listed in *Lloyd's Register* although no movements had been reported for several years.

Ben Vooar (3). *[J. and M. Clarkson]*

18. BEN VOOAR (3) 1959-1975
O.N. 184821 427g 218n 149.3 x 26.9 x 8.8 feet.
Brons oil engine 6-cyl. 2SCSA by N.V. Appingedammer Bronsmotorenfabriek, Appingedam; 375 BHP, 9 knots.
10.10.1950: Launched by E.J. Smit & Zoon Scheepswerven N.V., Westerbroek (Yard No. 717).
6.12.1950: Completed for S. Dost (Carebeka N.V., managers), Groningen, Holland as MUDO.
1958: Sold to Rederij 'Mudo' (Carebeka N.V., managers), Groningen.
7.1959: Acquired by the Ramsey Steamship Co. Ltd., Ramsey and renamed BEN VOOAR.
3.6.1975: Aground a quarter mile south east of Inishowen Head whilst bound for Portrush in ballast. Taken in tow by two fishing vessels and beached at Greencastle, County Donegal. Later towed into Londonderry and declared a constructive total loss.
7.1975: Sold by her underwriters to Le Blond Shipping Co., North Shields.
1976: Repaired and renamed ARRAN FIRTH.
1981: Sold to St. Ives Motor and Marine (Cornwall) Ltd., Baldock, Hertfordshire and registered in Panama.
1981: Sold to Sindbad Shipping Co., Dubai, United Arab Emirates and renamed SINDBAD VI.
1982: Sold to Mohammed Abdalla Al Kaabi, Dubai and renamed SUHAIL STAR.
14.7.1984: Struck submerged object and beached on the coast of Oman in position 21.25.12 north by 59.00.00 east. Subsequently declared a constructive total loss.

19. BEN VARREY (3) 1963-1985
O.N. 184822 451g 234n 170.4 x 27.6 x 10.5 feet.
Oil engine 8-cyl. 2SCSA by N.V. Appingedammer Bronsmotorenfabriek, Appingedam; 500 BHP.
10.11.1962: Launched by N.V. E. J. Smit and Zoon Scheepswerven, Westerbroek (Yard No. 769).
3.1963: Completed for the Ramsey Steamship Co. Ltd., Ramsey as BEN VARREY.
18.3.1963: Commenced trading.
14.12.1984: Towed into Ramsey with severe engine trouble.
1.8.1985: Sold for demolition to Duddon Valley Shipbreakers, Millom.
17.9.1985: Arrived Millom from Ramsey in tow of PRIMROSE.

Ben Varrey (3) with cargo gear removed. *[J.K. Byass]*

Ben Varrey (3) as built.*[J. and M. Clarkson]*

20. BEN VEG (2)   1965-1978
O.N. 184823 346g 151n 143.8 x 26.3 x 10.3 feet.
Oil engine 6-cyl. 4SCSA by Blackstone and Co. Ltd., Stamford; 495 BHP.
16.12.1964: Launched by Clelands Shipbuilding Co. Ltd., Wallsend (Yard No. 280).
3.3.1965: Completed for the Ramsey Steamship Co. Ltd., Ramsey as BEN VEG.
9.3.1965: Commenced trading.
1978: Laid up at Ramsey, having completed 930 voyages.
13.10.1978: Sold to the Tyne Shiprepair Group, South Shields and later renamed BENN.
1979: Owners became Brigham and Cowan Ltd., South Shields.

1980: Sold to the Interisland Shipping Co. (West Indies) Ltd., Grenada and transferred to the St. Vincent flag.

3/4.8.1980: Driven aground at Bridgetown, Bahamas, by Hurricane Allen.

9.8.1980: Refloated and towed to Georgetown.

9.1989: Towed from Venezuela to Trinidad for repairs. During welding work at Port of Spain, caught fire, damage being minor.

1.1991: Towed to Castries for further work. During heavy weather the towline broke, and the unmanned ship is presumed to have sunk.

21. BEN VEEN (2) 1971-1984

O.N. 307950 486g 274n 161.0 x 29.3 x 10.5 feet.
Oil engine 6-cyl. 4SCSA by W.H. Allen, Sons and Co. Ltd., Bedford; 540 BHP.

1.7.1965: Launched by Richards (Shipbuilders) Ltd., Lowestoft (Yard No. 482).

9.1965: Completed for the General Steam Navigation Co. Ltd.,

London as PLOVER.

19.11.1971: Acquired by the Ramsey Steamship Co. Ltd., Ramsey and renamed BEN VEEN.

30.11.1984: Sold to Captain B.W. Wells, Chatham and others.

3.1985: Owners became Totebourne Ltd. (Captain B.W. Wells), Chatham (Sully Freight Ltd., Norwich, managers) and renamed MEDINA D.

6.8.1986: Laid up at Gillingham.

1986: Sold to Captain J. Armstrong, Abingdon (Sully Freight Ltd., Great Yarmouth, managers).

1988: Managers deleted.

19.10.1988: Struck submerged object, capsized and sank in heavy weather south west of East Holm Buoy off Lowestoft whilst on a voyage from Rouen to Great Yarmouth with a cargo of grain.

Ben Veen (2) on 4th June 1976. *[J. and M. Clarkson]*

Ben Ain (2) loading grain. *[Company archives]*

22. BEN AIN (2) 1976-1991
O.N. 308078 500g 289n 55.94 x 8.72 x 3.97 metres.
Oil engine 6-cyl. 4SCSA by Blackstone and Co. Ltd., Stamford; 530 BHP, 10.5 knots.
18.2.1966: Launched by Boele's Scheepswerven & Machinefabriek N.V., Bolnes (Yard No. 1023).
3.1966: Completed for the Blue Star Line Ltd., London (G.T. Gillie and Blair Ltd., Newcastle-upon-Tyne, managers) as DEBEN.
1971: Sold to Mardorf, Peach and Co. Ltd., London (Gillie and Blair Ltd., Newcastle-upon-Tyne, managers) and renamed GRETCHEN WESTON.
1974: Management ceased.
13.1.1976: Acquired by the Ramsey Steamship Co. Ltd., Ramsey at the yard of James Lamont and Co. Ltd., Greenock.
19.1.1976: Registered at Ramsey as BEN AIN.
6.6.1991: Sold to Pike Ship Sales, London.
1991: Sold to Ptolemos Tlais, Limassol, Cyprus, renamed PRINCE and registered in San Lorenzo, Honduras.

1994: Sold to Seapride Shipping Co. Ltd, Limassol, Cyprus (J.B. Shipping Services, Beirut, Lebanon, managers).
1998: Sold to Mahmoud Ali Ibrahim, Tripoli, Lebanon, renamed ABDOULAH and later ABDOULAH 1 and registered in La Paz, Bolivia.
3.2003: Still listed in *Lloyd's Register*.

23. BEN VANE 1988-2001
O.N. 377475 499g 275n 50.17 x 8.95 x 4.32 metres.
Oil engine 6-cyl. 4SCSA TBD 440 type by Motorenwerke Mannheim A.G., Mannheim, West Germany; 700 BHP, 9.5 knots.
12.1977: Completed by Wroclawska Stocznia Rzeczna, Wroclaw, Poland (Yard No. B529/05) for the Julia Shipping Co. Ltd., Georgetown, Cayman Islands (Navimercantile Ltd., London, managers) as JULIA S.
8.8.1980: Sold to Scheepvaart Maatschappij Ewout B.V., Rotterdam, Holland.

Ben Vane without a funnel, 2nd November 1988. *[Roy Cripps]*

Above: *Ben Vane* with a funnel in September 1995 at Douglas.

Below: *Ben Ellan* (2) approaches Douglas, 17th June 1992.
[*Roy Cripps*].

1980: Sold to Golden Age Marine Ltd., Limassol, Cyprus and renamed BULK MOON.

1986: Managers became H. and M. Marine Services Ltd., Woking, Surrey.

1987: Sold to Sea Triumph Shipping Ltd. (H. and M. Marine Services Ltd., Woking, Surrey, managers) retaining Cyprus flag.

16.8.1988: Acquired by the Ramsey Steamship Co. Ltd., Ramsey and renamed BEN VANE.

27.7.2001: Sold to Clydeboyd (Fort William) Ltd., Glasgow and renamed BEN NEVIS.

3.2003: Still in service.

24. BEN ELLAN (2) 1990-

O.N. 398843 538g 276n 49.97 x 9.28 x 4.02 metres.

Oil engine 5-cyl. 4SCSA by Aabenraa Motorfabrik, H. Callesen A/S, Aabenraa, Denmark; 575 BHP.

2.6.1981: Launched by J.W. Cook and Co. (Wivenhoe) Ltd., Wivenhoe (Yard No. 1465).

8.1981: Completed for the General Freight Co. Ltd. (F.T. Everard and Sons Management Ltd., managers), London as RIVER TAMAR.

1985: Sold to Custodian Leasing Ltd., Croydon (Whitbury Shipping Co. Ltd., Sheerness, managers).

1986: Owner became Clientcare Ltd., Croydon (Whitbury Shipping Co. Ltd., Sheerness, managers).

15.11.1990: Acquired by the Ramsey Steamship Co. Ltd., Douglas, Isle of Man and renamed BEN ELLAN.

3.2003: In the present fleet.

Ben Maye (2) in the River Mersey, 26th August 1999.
[Jim McFaul]

25. BEN MAYE (2) 1995-

O.N. 386403 548g 249n 48.75 x 9.10 x 4.50 metres.
Oil engine 8-cyl. 4SCSA ESL-type by Mirrlees Blackstone (Stamford) Ltd., Stamford; 1,100 BHP, 10.5 knots.
15.11.19678: Launched by Bideford Shipyard (1973) Ltd., Bideford (Yard No. Y78).
3.1979: Completed for Cornish Shipping Ltd., Plymouth as PEROTO.
1981: Registered in Guernsey.
1991: Owners became Cornish Shipping (C.I.) Ltd. (Sanders, Stevens and Co. Ltd., managers), Plymouth, and registered in Gibraltar.
1994: Managers became W.D. Tamlyn and Co. Ltd., Plymouth.
1994: Renamed VENDOME.
24.4.1995: Arrested at Plymouth by Lloyd's Bank and offered for sale.
1995: Acquired by the Ramsey Steamship Co. Ltd., Douglas and renamed BEN MAYE.
3.2003: In the present fleet.

26. BEN VARREY (4) 1999-

O.N. 722827 997g 547n 63.84 x 11.71 x 4.83 metres.
Oil engine 6-cyl. 4SCSA Mu452AK-type by Krupp MaK. Maschinebau GmbH, Kiel, West Germany; 740 BHP, 10 knots.
8.1986: Launched by Bodewes Scheepswerven B.V., Hoogezand, Netherlands (Yard No. 552) for B.V. Globecka, B.V. Nobecka and B.V. Tribecka (Beck Scheepvaartkantoor B.V., managers), Groningen, Netherlands as TRIUMPH.
1998: Owners became Rederij Triumph.
1999: Acquired by the Ramsey Steamship Co. Ltd., Douglas and renamed BEN VARREY.
3.2003: In the present fleet.

Ben Varrey (4).

APPENDIX 1: SHIPS MANAGED BY J.B. KEE

Funnel: red, black top. Houseflag: none known.

1. LORD MILNER 1922-1924 Trawler
O.N. 117465 82g 34n 77.6 x 18.0 x 8.5 feet.
T. 3-cyl. by Crabtree and Co. Ltd., Great Yarmouth.
1909: C.2-cyl. by Crabtree and Co. Ltd., Great Yarmouth.
7.1903: Completed by the Selby Shipbuilding and Engineering Co. Ltd., Selby for the Lowestoft Steam Herring Drifters Co. Ltd., Lowestoft as LORD MILNER (LT 982).
1.1915: Hired by the Admiralty and served as a boom defence vessel, armed with a three-pounder gun.
1919: Returned to owners.
19.11.1920: Sold to the Admiralty.
10.4.1922: Acquired by John B. Kee, John T. Kee and Frederick Brew (John B. Kee, manager), Ramsey.
3.1.1924: Sold to T.W. Ward Ltd., Sheffield.
4.1934: Broken up by T.W. Ward Ltd., Preston, having been laid up at their yard for several years.
14.5.1934: Register closed.

2. PEMBREY 1923-1928
O.N. 130059 549g 242n 165.8 x 25.4 x 10.7 feet.
T. 3-cyl. by N.V. Industriele Maatschappij 'Hera', Ymuiden.
6.6.1920: Launched by Firma D. Boot, Alphen a/d Rijn.
9.1920: Completed for the Pembrey Steamship Co. Ltd. (Francis J. Evans, manager), Burry Port as PEMBREY.
31.1.1923: Owners became the Burryside Steamship Co. Ltd. (Francis J. Evans, manager), Burry Port.
16.6.1923: Sold to Alfred H. Connell, Liverpool.
21.7.1923: Acquired by the Island Steamship Co. Ltd. (John B. Kee, manager), Ramsey.
7.8.1928: Sold to the Société Belge d'Armament Maritime S.A., Antwerp, Belgium and renamed IDA.
22.9.1930: Wrecked in dense fog one cable west of Prawle Point whilst on a voyage from Cardiff to Portsmouth with a cargo of coal.
9.10.1930: Wreck broke in two and by November 1930 was virtually broken up.

3. LYD 1923-1924 Iron Dandy
O.N. 82017 117g 63n 83.4 x 17.6 x 8.5 feet.
C.2-cyl. by Hawthorns and Co., Leith.
1881: Launched by Hawthorns and Co., Leith (Yard No. 3) for J.W. Hope and Co., Leith as ANNIE HOPE.
1882: Sold to S.D. Davison, Leith.
13.3.1883: Ashore in gale near Holyhead whilst on a voyage from Bideford to Runcorn with a cargo of pipeclay. Later refloated.
1884: Sold to William H. Poole, Newcastle-upon-Tyne.
1885: Sold to John E. Crisp and Sons, Beccles and renamed JEANIE HOPE.
22.3.1906: Sold to the General Steam Navigation Co. Ltd., London.
30.1.1914: Sold to William Jones, Lydney, Gloucester.
9.1914: Renamed LYD.
24.12.1917: Sold to Leslie K. Osmond (Ernest Blow, manager), Hull.
12.2.1918: Owners became the Oberon Shipping Co. Ltd. (Ernest Blow, manager), Hull.
30.10.1918: Sold to the London Transport Co. Ltd. (Frank Newsom, manager), London.
12.4.1920: Manager became Ernest J. Heinz.
11.2.1921: Sold to Clelands (Ship Repairers) Ltd., Willington Quay-on-Tyne.
18.12.1923: Acquired by John B. Kee, Ramsey.
1.4.1924: Owners became John B. Kee, John T. Kee and Frederick Brew (John B. Kee, manager), Ramsey.
19.12.1924: Sold to John D. Ormiston, Leith.
14.10.1927: Sold to Peter C. MacLeod, Alloa.
1.4.1930: Sold to John Dutch, Perth.
12.8.1939: Owner became Ian A. Dutch, Perth.
28.8.1946: Sank off Perth Harbour in the River Tay whilst lying at anchor loading gravel and became a total loss.
14.11.1952: Register closed after she had been broken up.

Pembrey. [T.H. Midwood, Company archives]

Staffa. [Douglas Cochrane, World Ship Photo Library]

4. STAFFA 1925-1930

O.N. 99838 90g 35n 80.0 x 19.1 x 7.7 feet.
C. 2-cyl. by Muir and Houston, Glasgow.
7.1892: Completed by John Gilmour, Irvine for William Rafferty and John McKinney, Glasgow as NELLIE.
13.7.1903: Owner became William Rafferty, Glasgow.
19.2.1904: Sold to John W. McIntyre, Glasgow.
13.1.1908: Sold to David MacBrayne Ltd., Glasgow.
11.5.1910: Renamed STAFFA.
7.4.1916: Sold to Francis Reid, Ardrossan.

11.2.1925: Acquired by John B. Kee, John T. Kee and Frederick Brew (John B. Kee, manager), Ramsey.
25.11.1930: Sold to Osman J.N. Eynon, Angle, Pembroke.
28.4.1939: Sold to J.B. Le Page and Co. Ltd., Guernsey.
12.3.1942: Broke adrift and wrecked in Bray Harbour, Alderney whilst waiting to sail for Sark.

5. FAWN 1927-1940

O.N.105152 143g 49n 105.0 x 18.1 x 8.4 feet.
C.2-cyl. by Ross and Duncan, Glasgow.
7.1897: Launched by John Fullerton and Co., Paisley (Yard No. 137).
16.7.1897: Registered in the ownership of the St. Malo and Binic Steamship Co. Ltd. (J. Piprell and Sons, managers), Guernsey as FAWN.
7.5.1923: Sold to Donald Robertson, Glasgow.
2.6.1927: Acquired by John B. Kee, Ramsey.
12.12.1938: Owners became J.B. Kee (1930) Ltd. (J. Ramsay, manager), Ramsey.
16.5.1940: Sold to the Liverpool Derricking and Carrying Co. Ltd., Liverpool.
4.10.1940: Sold to the Norwest Construction Co. Ltd. (J.S. Baucher, manager), Liverpool.
6.11.1941: Sold to James C. Screech, Appledore.

Fawn. [World Ship Photo Library]

Bradda. [Douglas Cochrane, World Ship Photo Library]

12.1941-1945: Served as a Royal Navy degaussing vessel.
7.3.1942: Sold to the Kingsley Shipping and Storage Co. Ltd. (David S. Merrifield, manager), Appledore.
24.11.1947: Sold to the Wirral Shipping Co. Ltd., London.
9.3.1948: Owners became the Wirral Steamship Co. Ltd., London.
5.5.1948: Renamed WIRRAL CAPE.
12.3.1951: Demolition commenced at Thornaby-on-Tees by the Stockton Shipping and Salvage Co. Ltd.

6. JOLLY FRANK/BRADDA 1930-1936
O.N. 143329 239g 104n 107.7 x 21.8 x 9.9 feet.
C. 2-cyl. by N.V. van de Kuy & van de Ree, Rotterdam.
1918: Completed by N.V. van de Kuy & van de Ree, Rotterdam (Yard No.35) for N.V. Stoomvaart Maatschappij Feducia, Rotterdam, Holland as FEDUCIA.

10.7.1919: Sold to Leopold H.G. Walford, London and renamed JOLLY FRANK.
15.12.1919: Owners became Walford Lines Ltd. (Leopold Walford (London) Ltd., managers), London.
16.12.1930: Acquired by John B. Kee, Ramsey.
29.6.1931: Renamed BRADDA.
10.1.1936: Blown over revetment in a gale, capsized and sank near Formby Point in the River Mersey whilst on a voyage from Birkenhead to Rogerstown with a cargo of coal. There was only one survivor from her crew of six.

7. J.B. KEE 1936-1957
O.N. 143346 241g 97n
107.5 x 21.2 x 9.7 feet.
C. 2-cyl. by N.V. Werf Hubertina voor heen W.H. Jacobs, Haarlem.
1917: Completed by N.V. Werf Hubertina voor heen W.H. Jacobs, Haarlem (Yard No. 131) for J.W.F. Kools, Rotterdam, Holland as WILLY.
1919: Sold to Walford Lines Ltd. (G.P.Walford, manager), London and renamed JOLLY DIANA.
1920: Managers became Leopold Walford (London) Ltd.
1922: Sold to Walter Cowley, Port St. Mary.
1923: Renamed MONA'S BELLE.
1926: Sold to the Mona Steamship (1926) Ltd. (Joseph A. Qualtrough, manager), Port St. Mary.
1936: Acquired by J.B. Kee (1930) Ltd. (James Ramsay, manager), Ramsey and renamed J.B.KEE.
5.11.1957: Foundered near the entrance to the Rock Channel, Liverpool Bay after her cargo of gravel had shifted eleven miles west of Morecambe Light Vessel in heavy weather during a voyage from Ramsey to Liverpool. Her crew was rescued by the New Brighton Lifeboat which was escorting her at the time.

J.B. Kee. [J.K. Byass]

APPENDIX 2: DOUGLAS SHIPPING CO. LTD.

Funnel: red with three legs of Man in white, with letters DSC and black top. Houseflag: none known

1. E.D.J. 1916-1917 Steel auxiliary ketch
O.N.132756 76g 57n 67.1 x 18.0 x 7.8 feet.
Oil engine 3-cyl. 2SCSA by William Beardmore and Co. Ltd., Glasgow.
3.1914: Completed by Willoughby Brothers, Plymouth for their own account as E.D.J.
1915: Sold to the Western Counties Brick Co. Ltd., Plymouth.
1916: Acquired by the Douglas Shipping Co. Ltd. (George E. Kelly, manager), Douglas.
1917: Sold to John Henderson, Belfast.
1919: Sold to Thomas Pallister, William S. Blues and Thomas G.W. Clarke, Newcastle-upon-Tyne.
1921: Owner became William S. Blues, Newcastle-upon-Tyne.
1922: Sold to the Lower Shannon Shipping Co., Limerick.
1922: Sold to the Shannon Express Co. Ltd. (C.H. Power, manager), Limerick.
1925: Sold to the Shannon Steamship Co. Ltd., Kilrush.
c1947: Driven ashore at Aylevaroo in the Lower Shannon following an engine failure whilst on passage from Kilrush to Limerick with a cargo of turf. Subsequently refloated but not considered worth repairing, and sold to the Hammond Lane Metal Co. Ltd., Dublin for demolition.
21.8.1951: Register closed.

2. GLADYS 1916 Wooden ketch
O.N.86464 76g 62n 75.9 x 19.9 x 8.4 feet.
4.1894: Completed by David Banks and Co., Plymouth.
26.4.1894: Registered in the ownership of Thomas Mourant, Grouville, Jersey as GLADYS.
20.4.1916: Acquired by George E. Kelly, Douglas.
13.5.1916: Registered at Douglas.
30.5.1916: Owners became the Douglas Shipping Co. Ltd., Douglas.
24.10.1916: Stranded on rocks west south west of Douglas Head in a southerly gale whilst on a voyage from Manchester to Douglas with a cargo of coal. Her crew of four was lost.
7.11.1916: Register closed.

3. HARVEST HOME 1917 Wooden schooner
O.N.81238 103g 79n 88.4 x 21.4 x 9.6 feet.
10.1882: Launched by Peter Lund, Tarleton, Lancashire.
28.11.1882: Registered in the ownership of Thomas Ashcroft and others, Preston as HARVEST HOME.
23.8.1886: Managing owner becomes Joseph Taylor, Lathom, Lancashire.
12.1904: Sold to John Rooney, Kilkeel.
2.11.1908: Sold to Gregory Devereux, Wexford.
16.3.1917: Acquired by the Douglas Shipping Co. Ltd. (George E. Kelly, manager), Douglas.
28.3.1917: Captured by the German Submarine UC 65 and sunk by gunfire four miles north east of the South Arklow Lightvessel whilst on a voyage from Wexford to Garston with a cargo of timber.
25.4.1917: Register closed.

4. TEXA 1917-1931 Iron steamer
O.N.89961 157g 41n 100.0 x 19.1 x 8.8 feet.
1891: 185g 71n 118.4 x 19.1 x 8.8 feet.
C.2-cyl. by William King and Co., Glasgow; 35 NHP.
9.1884: Completed by Scott and Co., Bowling (Yard No. 54) for W. and J. Mutter, Glasgow as JAMES MUTTER.
1889: Sold to David MacBrayne, Glasgow and renamed TEXA.
15.4.1891: Re-registered after lengthening by the Ailsa Shipbuilding Co., Troon.
3.1.1906: Owners became David MacBrayne Ltd., Glasgow.
20.7.1917: Acquired by the Douglas Shipping Co. Ltd. (George E. Kelly, manager), Douglas.
5.11.1931: Sold to Samuel Gray, Belfast.
30.4.1932: Wrecked four miles from Ballyshannon whilst on a voyage from Preston to Ballyshannon with a cargo of coal.
21.9.1932: Register closed.

Texa. [Douglas Cochrane, World Ship Photo Library]

5. TREVOR 1919-1932

O.N.123989 196g 69n 106.0 x 22.0 x 8.9 feet.
C. 2-cyl. by W.J. Yarwood and Sons, Northwich; 30 NHP, 210 IHP, 8 knots.
14.1.1905: Commenced by W.J. Yarwood and Sons, Northwich (Yard No. 45).
27.7.1906: Completed.
7.8.1906: Registered in the ownership of the Trevor Steamship Co. Ltd. (Henry Seddon, manager), Liverpool as TREVOR.
11.1.1919: Acquired by the Douglas Shipping Co. Ltd.

(George E. Kelly, manager), Douglas, Isle of Man.
19.9.1930: Manager became Leonard M. Callow.
28.4.1932: Sold to Stephen A. Portus, Garston.
4.5.1932: Sold to William N. George, Llanelly.
27.2.1933: Owner became Gaynor George, Llanelly.
21.6.1934: Sold to Coppack Brothers and Co., Connah's Quay.
30.7.1937: Register closed after being broken up on Tranmere Beach.

Trevor. [J. and M. Clarkson]

APPENDIX 3: SHIPS MANAGED FOR R.A.COLBY CUBBIN

These vessels were managed by the Ramsey Steamship Company on behalf of the owners.

1. GROSVENOR 1940-1946

O.N.140824 305g 114n 130.8 x 22.6 x 9.8 feet.
C. 2-cyl. by Gauldie and Gillespie, Glasgow.
20.10.1921: Launched by Ritchie, Graham and Milne, Whiteinch, Glasgow (Yard No. 375).
1.1922: Completed.
23.3.1922: Registered in the ownership of the Moffat Steamship Co. Ltd. (Moffat and Nickerson, managers), Grimsby as ELIZABETH MOFFAT.
20.11.1922: Sold to the Thomas Brothers Shipping Co. Ltd., Liverpool.
27.11.1922: Renamed ELSIE THOMAS.
28.10.1930: Owners became Thomas Coasters Ltd., Liverpool.

13.1.1936: Sold to Alexander M. Massie, Aberdeen.
11.3.1936: Renamed GROSVENOR.
7.1.1937: Sold to W.N. Lindsay Ltd., Leith.
12.7.1940: Acquired by Mrs. Ellen M.M.G. Cubbin (R.A. Colby Cubbin, manager), Douglas, Isle of Man.
6.12.1946: Sold to the Estuary Shipping Co. Ltd., Leith.
10.4.1948: Renamed CRAIG.
27.7.1948: Sold to Norman Stewart, Leith.
7.1952: Arrived at Gateshead for breaking up by C.W. Dorkin and Co.
23.4.1953: Register closed.

Grosvenor with her later name Craig. [E. Dewulf-Pott]

Kyle Rhea. [J. and M. Clarkson]

2. KYLE RHEA 1940-1955
See BEN MAYE, number 16 in the Ramsey Steamship list.

INDEX OF SHIPS' NAMES

Names in CAPITALS are those carried when in the Ramsey Steamship or other fleet featured in this book.

Abdoulah	40	BEN VEG (1)	5-8,10,14,26,27	Gretchen Weston	22,40	PEMBREY	8,43
Abdoulah 1	40	BEN VEG (2)	3,21,22,25,38,39	GROSVENOR	47	Peroto	23,42
Agia Moni	37	BEN VOOAR (1)		HARVEST HOME	46	Plover	22,39
Annie Hope	43		7,8,10,12,13,28,29	Ida	43	President, HMS	14
Ardgowan	5	BEN VOOAR (2)		Isabel	6	Primrose	38
Arran Firth	22,37		13,14,16,32,33	J.B. KEE	13,14,16,18,45	Ready	30
Ashdene	34	BEN VOOAR (3)	19,21-23,37	James Mutter	46	Redstone	7,29
Athelrill	30	Benn	39	Jeanie Hope	43	River Tamar	23,41
Beaconia	16,17,35	BRADDA	13,45	Johan	27	Sarah Blanche	9,30
BEN AIN (1)	2,14,16,21,33	Britannia	7	Jolly Basil	9,30	Sea Explorer II	27
BEN AIN (2)	22,23,40	Brittany	14,27	Jolly Diana	45	Sindbad VI	37
BEN BLANCHE	9-11,13,30	Bulk Moon	23,41	JOLLY FRANK	45	STAFFA	9,44
BEN ELLAN (1)	13,14,19,32	Bullger	36	Julia S	40	Starling	7,27
BEN ELLAN (2)	23,24,41	Burscough	10	Kaponas TH	37	Stertpoint	34
BEN JEE (1)	10,11,30,31	Cargan	13,33	Kyle Rhea	16,36,48	Suhail Star	37
BEN JEE (2)	15,16,34,35	Coombe Dingle	13	Limesfield	27	Tamara	16,18,37
BEN MAY	10,11,30,31	Craig	47	Lise EG	27	Tern	7,29
BEN MAYE (1)	16,17,21,22,36	CROSSBILL	14,15,34	Lita	37	TEXA	7,10,46
BEN MAYE (2)	42	Deben	40	Lorbas	27	Tod Head	36
Ben Nevis	41	Dennis Head	14,32	LORD MILNER	8,43	TREVOR	6,7,10,47
BEN REIN (1)	6,7,9,24,26,27	Deveson	7,29	Lossie	35	Triumph	24,42
BEN REIN (2)	7,8,9, 28,29	Doris Thomas	32	LYD	9,43	UB 57	7,27
BEN REIN (3)	18,21,22,36,37	E.D.J.	46	Manx Fairy	4	Vendome	23,42
BEN SEYR		Elidir	16	Marche Droit	30	War Deveron	29
	7,8,10,11,13,14,16,29	Elizabeth Moffat	47	Medina D	39	War Lossie	35
BEN VANE	23,24,40,41	Elsie Thomas	47	Mia	35	WHITESTONE	6,7,27
BEN VARREY (1)		FAWN	9,14,44	Molarill	30	Willy	45
	1,6,8,10,14,15,27	Feducia	45	Mona's Belle	13,45	Wirral Cape	45
BEN VARREY (2)	16-18,35	Gianna P	37	Moorside	32	Wyre Revenge	21
BEN VARREY (3)	20-22,38	GLADYS	46	Mudo	19,37	Yarmouth Trader	15,34
BEN VARREY (4)	24,25,42	Glenmay	10,30	Nellie	44		
BEN VEEN (1)	15,21,34	Glentow	5	Norman	7,27		
BEN VEEN (2)	22,39	Gloucesterbrook	27	Pegrix	13,32		

ART NOUVEAU TILES

c. 1890-1914

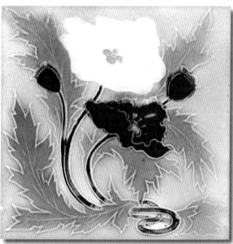
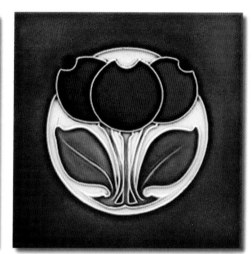

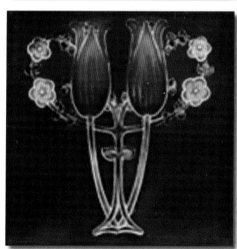

Schiffer Publishing Ltd®

4880 Lower Valley Road, Atglen, PA 19310 USA

SANDIE FOWLER & WENDY HARVEY
OF ANTIQUE ARTICLES

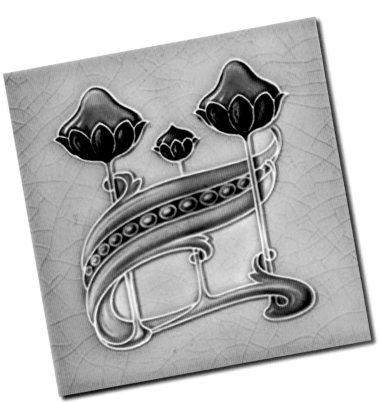

Dedication

This book is dedicated to all who started out as our customers and who now we call our friends.
Thanks for all your encouragement and enthusiasm.

Library of Congress Cataloging-in-Publication Data

Fowler, Sandra, 1937-
Art nouveau tiles c. 1890-1914 / by Sandie Flwler & Wendy Harvey.
p. cm.
 ISBN 0-7643-1441-6
1. Tiles. 2. Decoration and ornament--Art nouveau. I. Harvey, Wendy.
II. Title.
NK4670 .F74 2001
738.6'075--dc21
2001003936

Designed by Bonnie M. Hensley
Cover design by Bruce M. Waters
Type set in Benguiat Bk BT/Korinna BT

ISBN: 0-7643-1441-6
Printed in China
1 2 3 4

Published by Schiffer Publishing Ltd.
4880 Lower Valley Road
Atglen, PA 19310
Phone: (610) 593-1777; Fax: (610) 593-2002
E-mail: Schifferbk@aol.com
Please visit our web site catalog at
www.schifferbooks.com

This book may be purchased from the publisher.
Include $3.95 for shipping. Please try your bookstore first.
We are always looking for people to write books on new and related subjects. If you have an idea for a book please contact us at the above address.
You may write for a free catalog.

In Europe, Schiffer books are distributed by
Bushwood Books
6 Marksbury Avenue
Kew Gardens
Surrey TW9 4JF England
Phone: 44 (0) 20-8392-8585; Fax: 44 (0) 20-8392-9876
E-mail: Bushwd@aol.com
Free postage in the UK. Europe: air mail at cost.

Contents

Introduction 4
Chapter 1: Art Nouveau 7
Chapter 2: Tile Collecting 12
Chapter 3: Tile Companies and Their Wares 16
    T. & R. Boote, Ltd. 16
    W. & E. Corn Brothers 28
    Craven Dunnill & Company 34
    Doulton & Company, Ltd. 35
    Gibbons Hinton & Company 36
    Godwin & Hewitt; Godwin & Thynne 38
    H. & R. Johnson, Ltd. 40
    Lee & Boulton 43
    Malkin Edge & Company 45
    Marsden Tile Company; Maw & Company 47
    Alfred Meakin & Company 48
    Mintons China Works 52
    Minton, Hollins & Company 54
    H.A. Ollivant 56
    Pilkingtons Tile & Pottery Company, Ltd. 58
    Rhodes Tile Company 68
    H. Richards Tile Company 69
    Sherwin & Cotton 84
    Miscellaneous Tile Companies 90
Unattributed Tile Manufacturers 93
Four Square Designs 152
Transfer Tiles by Various Makers 156
Art Nouveau Water Lily Tiles 159
Tube-lined Tiles 163
Spacer Tiles 168
German Tiles 176
Belgium Tiles 184
Bibliography 191

Introduction

I started collecting and buying antiques about 1973. Somewhere around 1980 I started to buy and sell at local antique and flea markets. The antique bug had somehow infected me. Buying all these old and wonderful curious items of yesterday became a great pastime. There was a lot of fun in finding the items and doing the research to learn more about what they were and what value they had in the collecting marketplace.

It was about 1988 when Wendy joined me in this business. We would go to auctions and buy box lots of items. It was so exciting to see what treasures we had that we would spend hours going through boxes and washing the item, researching, and then preparing to take them to the marketplace. We would set up at a local market every Sunday. Then we got involved with antique co-ops and having our items on display on a regular basis. We were working toward having this become a viable business that, hopefully, would support us someday and allow time for travel. We started to do larger markets and started following the antique show circuit. Wendy was very instrumen-

tal in us traveling and in choosing to do larger and more specialized markets. She would set goals and encourage me to take the risks. We would buy just about anything that we liked and we thought we could sell. In 1990 I left my full time job and dedicated all of my time to this business of ours.

It was in the summer of 1992 that we stumbled upon a treasure that would take us on a wonderful journey that continues today. We were in a shop in Stowe, Vermont when we found four Wedgwood tiles in pink and white transfer from the month series designed by Helen Miles, each representing a different month. They were very charming and Wendy fell in love with them. It was quite a bit later that we found out how rare these particular tiles were.

In the fall of 1992 we took a vacation in London. This trip was a major turning point for us. We visited the Victoria & Albert Museum and viewed their tile room. It was an absolutely amazing experience to see the variety of tiles and all of the dif-

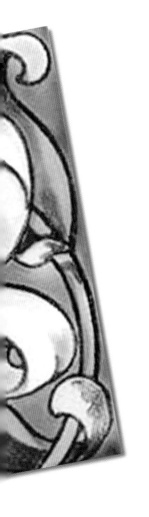

ferent styles, designs, and techniques. Learning about the ceramic surface was something that we definitely wanted to pursue. We viewed as much as we possibly could during that week in London. We also shopped all of the flea markets with the hope of finding tiles to purchase. I believe that we bought twenty-five tiles on that trip. We also bought as many books as we could find so that we could start to learn as much as possible. Unfortunately, there were not many books specific to tiles at that point, but our library has grown considerably since then. That trip was one of our very best as it was the beginning of a new journey in life. A simple vacation turned into a love affair.

One of the greatest joys of dealing with tiles has been the shared experience with the tile collectors that we have met over the years. We are members of the *Tile and Architectural Ceramics Society* in the UK, *The Tile Heritage Foundation*, *The Friends of Terra Cotta* and *The American Art Pottery Association* in the USA. We have met hundreds of people who are as excited about the tile surface as we are. All of these people have been friendly and willing and eager to share their experiences as well as their collections. They have told us about tile sites that are not to be missed, and museums and exhibitions where we could view some of the very best examples of tiles. They have invited us into their homes to share their collections. They have also supported and encouraged us in our pursuit to be one of the premier tile dealers here in the US. We are very grateful to all of these people who have touched our lives on this journey.

Our travels have taken us across the ocean to England many times. We have countless good memories of the friends who have opened their doors and invited us to sit down to tea and talk about tiles. They have shown us books, periodicals, and reference materials and have shared their knowledge with us. They have shown us tiles we could only hope to see on those visits. They have eagerly assisted us with directions and recommendations in our quest to find reclaimed tiles as we travel throughout small, quaint villages and large urban cities. Their friendship and enthusiasm is an integral piece of our business and this project.

I decided right in the beginning that if I was going to sell these beautiful pieces of decorative art, I had better take pictures of them so that I would at least be able to continue to view them after they were gone. I was never quite sure what would come of all of these images. However, We believe the time has come to share them with others who love tile and may not have had the opportunity to view quite as many examples as we have collected over the years.

Sometimes people will ask which tile is our favorite. Both Wendy and I reply the same way. It's the one that we are holding right now. It is so difficult to make comparisons. There were so many different designs, styles, and even techniques. It is absolutely fascinating to see all of that. However, in the past few years I have really fallen in love with the Art Nouveau style. This movement started in the late 1880s and moved into the 20th century. There were hundreds of designs done by dozens of different manufacturers. Sometimes, one company would copy the same design from another. This was often a result of certain artists leaving one company and joining another, but it was also a result of poor copyright laws at the time. Still, we are always amazed at how many different designs were produced. We are very intrigued with seeing the same design done in many different color combinations. It is also very exciting when we find tiles that we have never seen before.

We have chosen to show you images of the Art Nouveau time frame in this book. In some of these images you will see its roots in Victorian design, and in others the image will flow into the Art Deco period with its angular lines. We will be using a loose interpretation of the Art Nouveau style. We will also be giving you a loose range of dating for most tiles. We do not have access to original tile catalogs, which would be very beneficial for specific dates for particular designs. Many of the designs were made and continued for a period of several years, which would make a specific date rather difficult to determine. A few good books, which will help with dating tiles, are: *Victorian Ceramic Tiles* by Julian Barnard; *The Decorated Tile* by J & B Austwick; and *Collecting Victorian Tiles* by Terence A. Lockett.

The sole purpose of this book is to bring you the collector, dealer, historian, or just the casual observer, a visual treat. We have done our best to identify the tiles by the companies that produced them. In some cases the same design may be identified as being done by more than one company. This is because we have had that particular design on different tile backs. There were

cases of some companies buying the blanks from other companies and then doing the decoration. Unfortunately, there will be many tile images here that we cannot attribute to any particular company. In the beginning the image was more important than the details of manufacture. Our record keeping has become better over the years. However, there are many tiles that do not have enough information on the back of them for us to attribute them for sure. In the long run we think that you will agree that the tile design is what really counts.

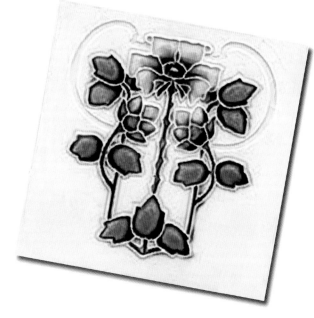

We believe that all of these images will prove to be a priceless piece of our visual heritage. We can only imagine how beautiful many of these tiles were in their original installations. Here we are viewing a single tile design, but originally they were never meant to stand alone as a single entity. Rather, they were to be part of the larger picture, the whole installation, the complete fireplace surround or the backsplash in a piece of furniture. There was continuity in the whole. We are grateful for the installations that are still *in situ*. We strongly believe they should stay intact for all to enjoy. However, we are just as grateful for all the single tiles that have been rescued from demolition. The whole would never be without the single pieces. We hope you will enjoy the images of what we believe were and still are a beautiful art form.

Art Nouveau

It is difficult to try and define or clarify exactly what Art Nouveau is in a short introduction. Art Nouveau was a dramatic decorative art movement that strived to change the traditional decorative styles. It was a transition period for the artists of the day. It was complex and took on many forms. It was an ornamental and decorative style not seen before the last two decades of the 19th century.

Complicating its definition, Art Nouveau styles underwent subtle changes from one company to another. That difference in style was even more noticeable depending on the country of origin. The interpretation may have been similar, but the styles varied.

The Art Nouveau style was generally characterized by organic, sinuous lines and animated curves. It was sometimes said to be narcissistic in style because of the sensuality of those lines and curves. It utilized rhythmic lines and rows of repeating or identical patterns. This, and its use of ornament, evoked the feeling of a flowing movement in the design, which sometimes seemed to change direction. Usually this resulted in the design filling a good portion of the tile surface. In contrast, there were many designs that remained small, leaving the background of the tile intentionally empty of design. This allowed the viewer to take in the effect of the translucent glaze. In many cases the ambiguity of design and its background were very typical of Art Nouveau. Many of these designs remained abstract forms to the casual observer.

The style and decorative themes were often taken from many natural sources. The most common was the plant, which symbolized organic life and offered endless expressions of living movement. Art Nouveau designers favored a floral bloom that could be interpreted two-dimensionally. Flowers with long, linear stems were popular, such as the lily, tulip, orchids, daisy, sunflower, and the iris. Water lilies were also much used among the designs found in this period. In many cases the simplest flower became elegant,

Spectacular tile panel done on four 8" tiles. The panel measures 8" x 32". It has been attributed to Leon Victor Solon while working at Mintons as their art director. You will rarely see Art Nouveau tiles done on an 8" tile and panels are extremely hard to find and much sought after.

with all of the curves, intertwining of the stems, and the bending of the flower this way or that, things never seen in the natural form. There were endless varieties of lines and shapes that could be taken from plant life and utilized in the expression of Art Nouveau.

Designs from nature have always been a source for the new artist as well as the experienced. The Art Nouveau movement gave artists the opportunity to adapt these designs and be creative with their form. It was an opportunity to be part of a progressive style. These design styles were also applied to birds and insects, as well as to female forms. Young women with long sensuous flowing hair were often used, most notably by Johann von Schwarz of Nürnberg, Germany. Unfortunately, there are few examples of this type of tile left for the collector to acquire in today's market place.

Our focus will be on the English Art Nouveau tiles. England was the major force in the development of the Art Nouveau tile, beginning its dominance in decoration around 1895 and continuing until around 1914. Many of the other European countries followed suit. Belgium was one of the major manufacturers of Art Nouveau tiles, even though they did not have tile production of any kind until about 1895. Belgium Art Nouveau designers expressed a complete originality in their designs. German designers also produced their fair share of wonderful designs. We will show you a small sampling of tiles from other countries for a visual comparison.

There was a very large demand for tiles at the end of the last century as a result of the industrial revolution. Mass pro-

Extraordinary tile plaque of a young woman done by the company of, Johann von Schwarz of Nürnberg, Germany, c1900, designed by Carl Siegmund Luber. It measures 11" by 6-1/2". Plaques such as these are very difficult to find.

Opposite page:
Beautiful Belgium four tile panel of a heron done by S.A. Manufactures Cèramiques d' Hemixem, Gilliot & Cie, Hemiksem, c1900. The panel measures 6" x 24".

9

duction meant that all, not just the wealthy, could enjoy decorated tiles. There was a tide of appreciation for this decorated element of architecture. Tiles were used to decorate and adorn the facades of buildings. They were used inside as well, where tiles covered entire walls in kitchens, baths, foyers, etc. and were used in fireplaces as well as on furniture. They were utilized in private homes and municipal buildings. Tile artists, manufacturers' patterns and designs, and the rich wonderful glazes created a visual attraction and added important elements of form and color to the surroundings of common people.

The new designs and color schemes of the Art Nouveau movement that grew out of the push toward modernism in the late 19th century, brought visual pleasure to the people in a very big way. In the late 20th and now into the 21st century, Art Nouveau tiles are being seen and treasured once again by throngs of collectors and appreciators of this beautiful ceramic art form.

While Art Nouveau tiles brought many new designs to the marketplace, the techniques of manufacture and decoration remained the same for many years. The vast majority of Art Nouveau tiles were mass produced by machine pressing. The embossed or impressed design was the most cost effective method. The tiles were pressed by a machine into a mold, saving the time of individual handwork. It will be this type of tile that today's collector will be most likely to find. The machine pressed tiles were usually finished with a majolica glaze, but you will occasionally find a transfer printed tile with the Art Nouveau motif. The application of the majolica glaze, however, seemed to emphasize the design and its dimensionality in a more effective manner.

Tube-lined tiles are some of the most coveted tiles by today's collectors. Examples of this technique are much more difficult to find. These were produced by a technique of delicate hand decoration where the raised lines of slip clay were drawn onto the tile, much like decorating a cake. The seams separated the areas of the colored glazes. The lines would be thin and tend to be more raised than those in the pressed tiles. In tube-lined tiles you can also see where the lines ended because you can generally see a small bubble or blob of slip where the nozzle had been lifted. Skilled artists applied this technique more often in the decoration of panels and murals. This is one reason we do not see an abundance of individual tiles. However, tube-lined tiles were made as single tiles and were very popular right around 1900. As a result of their popularity many pressed tiles were made to emulate the tube-lined technique. The collector should be aware of this and learn the differences between pressed and tube-lined tiles. The trained eye will certainly see the difference. Occasionally tube-lined tiles can still be found and will normally command a premium price in today's market.

This wonderful vertical panel is done with five 6" tiles. The main panel measures 6" x 30" plus border tiles. This panel is done with the tube-lined technique. It is mounted on a board so we are unable to see the reverse of the tile to identify the manufacturer.

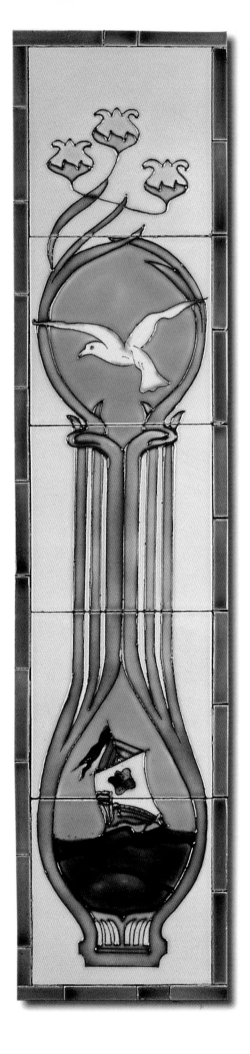

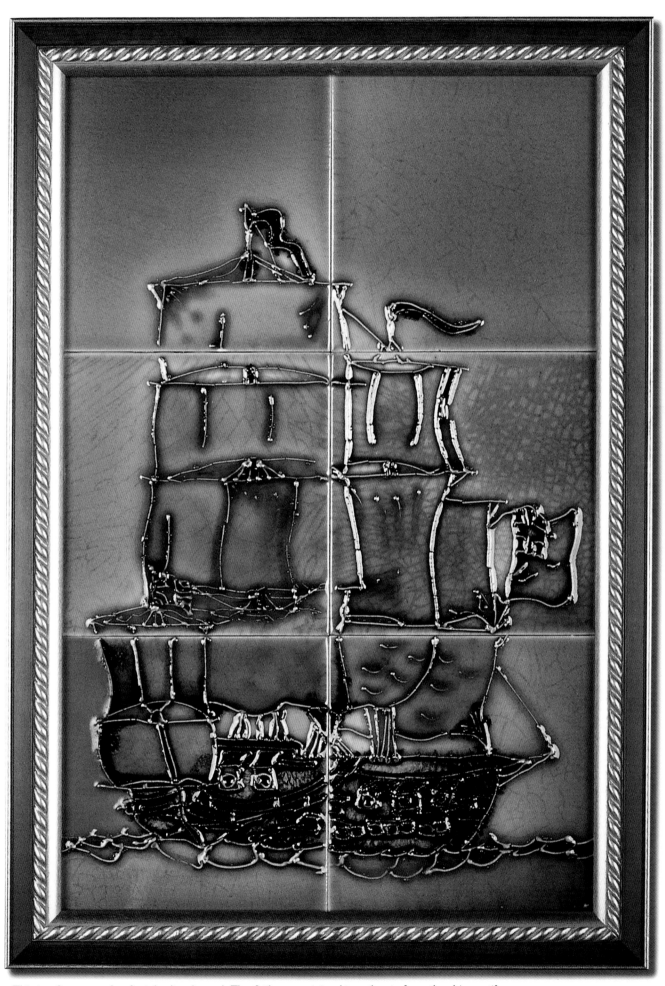

This is a fine example of a tube-lined panel. The 6 tiles were joined together to form the ship motif seen here. The panel was produced at Minton Hollins & Company. It measures 12" x 18".

Tile Collecting

We have been selling antique tile for the past 10 years. It might seem that this is a new area of collecting and it certainly is for many collectors. However, in our travels we have met collectors who have been avidly collecting examples for over 30 years. Certainly in this, as in all areas of collecting, there seems to be resurgence in interest among the new collector for any good design. A good design will always be a good design and a collector will continue to appreciate it for the same reasons other collectors were attracted to it throughout the years.

The reasons any individual is drawn to tile collecting are as varied as in any other area, and as always, individual preference is the key to collecting tiles. Historians, other collectors, or tile dealers cannot dictate what should or should not be collected as the best tiles. There is a very large range of designs and subject matter. Generally, after the first few purchases a collector will begin to focus their attention on a specific area of interest. This will normally allow them to refine their personal taste and at the same time become more knowledgeable about the types of tiles found in their own area of collecting. Once the collector gains more knowledge they are better able to find the prize as well as an occasional bargain.

We have seen a dramatic increase in the price of and interest in tiles over the last decade. For many years tiles were a relatively inexpensive collectible, with the exception of large or rare artist-attributed pieces. As more people have become exposed to tiles this has changed.

With the advent of the computer age it is changing again. The computer has allowed everyone to view tile images, tile sites, and museum collections from around the world. It has allowed many thousands of people to enjoy viewing a wide variety of beautiful tile images and to gather knowledge and information without leaving home.

As familiarity with tile design has increased so has the

interest in tile collecting. As always in any marketplace, the market price or value of a particular item is determined by those who wish to acquire it. An individual will determine how much they are willing to pay for a tile they want to add to their collection. In order to make an informed decision about the value of a tile the collector should know as much as possible about their purchase. It is also always a good idea to know the dealer you are buying from. If you can find a dealer who specializes in your collecting field you will reap the extra rewards of their expertise as well as finding a consistent source for new acquisitions.

It is also helpful for collectors to determine their own collecting style and ultimate collecting goal. It may be more important for you to have many items in your collection or you may choose to have fewer items of greater value or rarity. Regardless of your style, an important note for any collector is to buy the very best example you can for your money. Buying a tile simply because it is inexpensive is not necessarily the best reason and may not enhance the collection. However, if the tile design is rare or appealing then buying damaged may still be a good idea.

Here in the United States, clean and relatively good condition Art Nouveau tiles will range anywhere from around $85 to $165 or more depending on design and condition. Some of the simple four-square decorated designs will run about $35 to $55. Transfer Art Nouveau designs, which are more rare but generally less sought after, will be less money than press-molded or tube-lined tiles. Half tiles or spacer tiles that measure 3" x 6" should command less than a 6"

tile of similar design.

Good condition should be determined by having little to no surface wear and very few minor edge chips. It will be very rare to find tiles that are absolutely perfect, as most of them were used in installations. Many tiles have had their corners cut at a very slight angle to accommodate their installation. This should not be considered as damage and should not affect the integrity of the tile or its price. Original tiles can be found in extremely good condition when they have been cared for and not abused. The final value of any tile will be determined by the availability and how many collectors are vying to add it to their collection. Please remember that a price guide is simply that, just a guide and there are many variables.

Tile design also helps to determine pricing. There are many tile designs that you will see over and over again. Then a tile will appear that has not been seen in any of the books and all of the collectors will want to add it to their collection. The attribution of the design to a certain known artist is also a key factor. Supply and demand will always be a major component of pricing. Impulse to own is another factor that feeds the marketplace. Additionally many people are going back to tile installations in their homes. Many want the historical accuracy, design elements and the glaze richness of the original tiles. Original tile prices to date compare favorably to that of good quality new tiles.

There is a pretty consistent range of prices that have been established over the past few years. Inconsistencies will come into play when watching sales that take place on the Internet. On any particular day you may see a tile sell for $185 and then the following week a duplicate tile may sell for $65 or in some cases receive no bids at all. Often you can get a bargain, but the problem will always be in knowing if you are dealing with a credible person and knowing the condition of the tile you are buying. Generally you are not dealing with a specialist whose sole expertise is antique tile. As a result, there will be inconsistencies in the descriptions and many varied ideas of what good condition is. Some sellers will describe a tile as in good condition and it will actually have lots of damage. Some sellers will allude to the fact that a tile being 100 years old will allow damage to be excused. The fact is that a hundred year old tile can look exactly like a brand new tile out of the kiln if it has been handled properly and taken care of over the years. Fired clay, in reality, is very durable and will retain its vibrancy of color. Tiles do not fade from age or exposure to the sun. Generally crazing is a result of the firing process and has nothing to do with the age of the tile.

Many times tiles on the internet are misidentified, by company, date, or process. In some cases new reproduction tiles are being sold as originals. There are many individual sellers who simply do not have the expertise to describe a tile accurately. The remedy for dealing with these inconsistencies is to arm yourself with as much knowledge as possible before jumping into the bidding. Try to cultivate relationships with the people who are selling tiles. The rewards can be good for both buyer and seller.

Displaying Your Tiles

Seeing how many of the collectors have used and displayed their tiles has been a lot of fun for us. The experience has allowed us to enjoy their collections as well as learn from example so that we might share with other collectors. The most frequent question we are asked by the new collector or casual enthusiast is, "What do people do with these tiles?" We try to share the thoughts other collectors have shared with us. Many people will frame the tile as a piece of art. This can be a single piece or multiple tiles framed together. Others will sometimes use a wire plate rack to hang them so as not to detract from the tile at all. Some collectors will line bookshelves and others have had special racks built specifically to display groupings of tiles. You can use a simple or decorative easel and place them around to your liking anywhere in your home. Tiles work especially well in small spaces such as on narrow walls between doorways, over windows and doorjambs or perched on chair rails, moldings, and mantels. We have collectors that have them in kitchen counter tops and installed as a backsplash behind sinks and stoves. Many people use them to restore, replace, or build new installations around fireplaces. Tiles can be used in any room in the house to add a little color and interest.

When people are considering installation of antique tiles we always suggest that they place them in such a way that

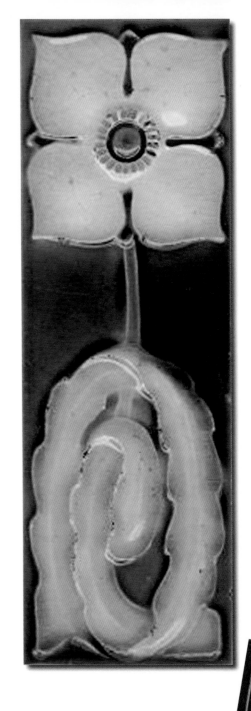

they can be easily removed again if desired. This would mean not using a heavy-duty cement to install them. Consult your tile setter for an adhesive product that will work for your purpose. A wood molding could also be used to secure them in place. We even know people who will hang tiles in place with Velcro and it works very well.

One of our favorite stories comes from an avid collector of Art Nouveau tiles. It goes something like this:

"I have all my tiles hanging in a rather strange place in my home. Many visitors to my home do not easily view the tiles. They are on a dark wall, but when I open my bedroom door every morning they are right in front of me and it makes me start my day with a smile by viewing something that brings me a great deal of pleasure."

That says it all; you buy tiles and collect because you have fallen in love with certain designs that bring you pleasure. At that point you can do whatever you want to display your found treasure. The best vantage point can only be decided by you. Once you have started collecting, you will decide what the very best way to display your tiles in your own space will be.

Art Nouveau tiles have provided us with countless hours of visual pleasure and joy. We are always delighted by the discovery of "new" designs and color combinations. We hope this book will expose even more people to the beauty of Art Nouveau tiles. We further hope that our enthusiasm for the tile surface will encourage others to appreciate this wonderful decorative art form from an influential style movement of a past era. We want to wish all of you who read this book, both the new collector and the veteran collector, many hours of pleasure from viewing these beautiful images of Art Nouveau designs.

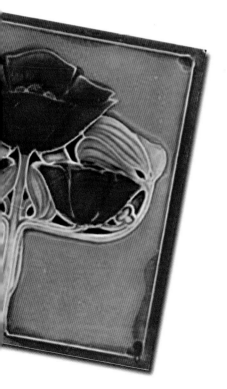

Tile Companies and Their Wares

T. & R. Boote, Ltd.

T. & R. Boote, Ltd. manufactured tiles from 1862 -1910. They were located in Burslem, Staffordshire. They were a major manufacturer of Art Nouveau tiles.

All of these tiles were done by T. & R. Boote , Ltd. They are all 6" tiles in very good condition. $100-$125.

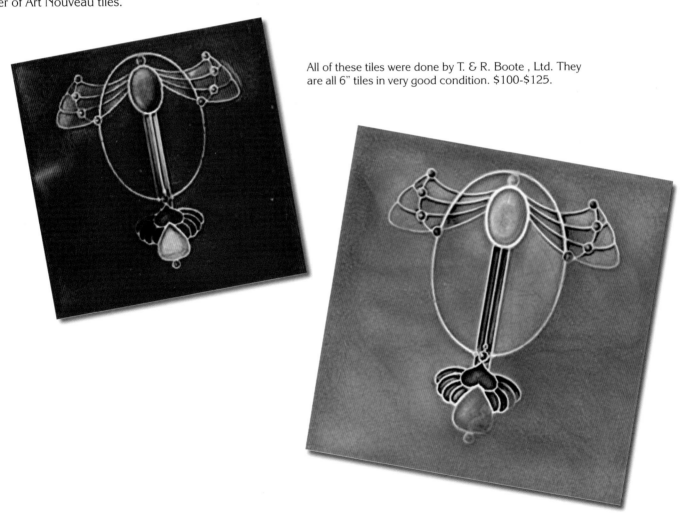

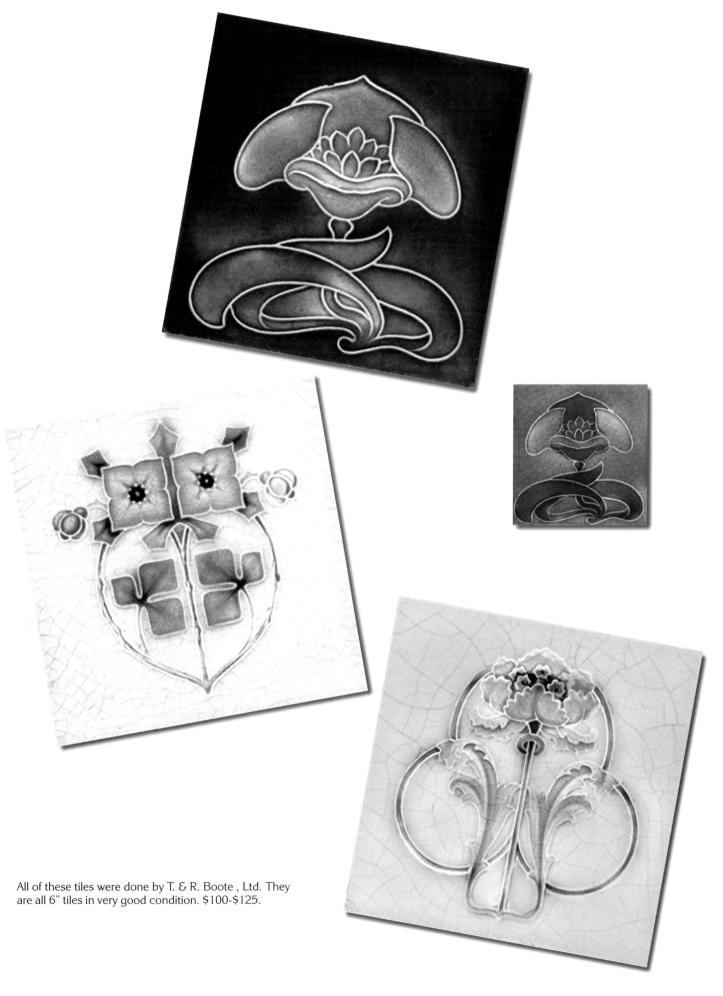

All of these tiles were done by T. & R. Boote , Ltd. They are all 6" tiles in very good condition. $100-$125.

All of these tiles were done by T. & R. Boote , Ltd. They are all 6" tiles in very good condition. $100-$125.

18

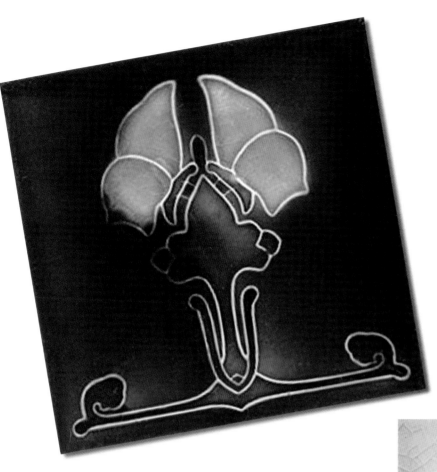

All of these tiles were done by T. & R. Boote , Ltd. They are all 6" tiles in very good condition. $100-$125.

All of these tiles were done by T. & R. Boote , Ltd. They are all 6" tiles in very good condition. $100-$125.

All of these tiles were done by T. & R. Boote , Ltd. They are all 6" tiles in very good condition. $100-$125.

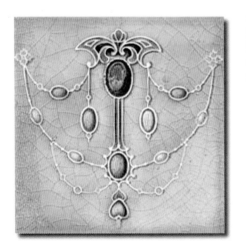

All of these tiles were done by T. & R. Boote , Ltd. They are all 6" tiles in very good condition. $100-$125.

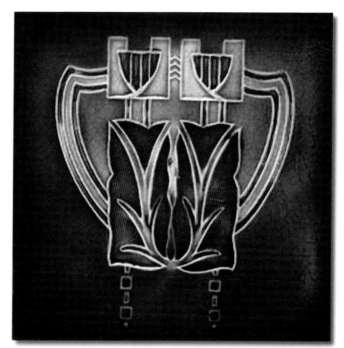

All of these tiles were done by T. & R. Boote , Ltd. They are all 6" tiles in very good condition. $100-$125.

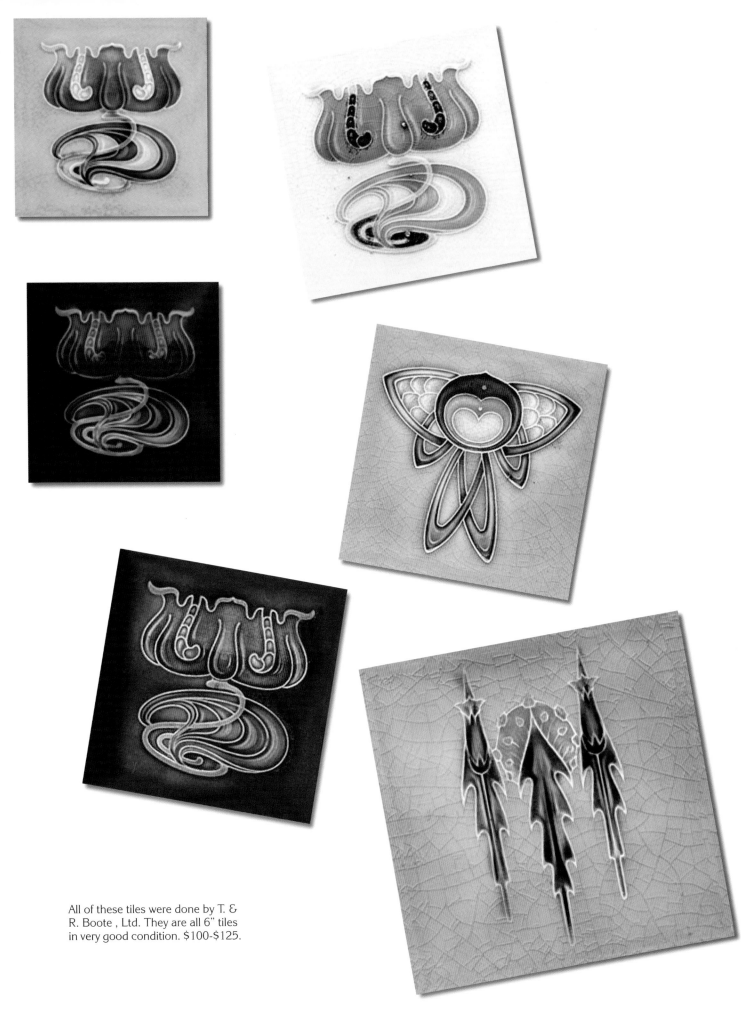

All of these tiles were done by T. &
R. Boote , Ltd. They are all 6" tiles
in very good condition. $100-$125.

24

All of these tiles were done by T. & R. Boote , Ltd. They are all 6" tiles in very good condition. $100-$125.

All of these tiles were done by T. & R. Boote , Ltd. They are all 6" tiles in very good condition. $100-$125.

All of these tiles were done by T. & R. Boote , Ltd. They are all 6" tiles in very good condition. $85-$100.

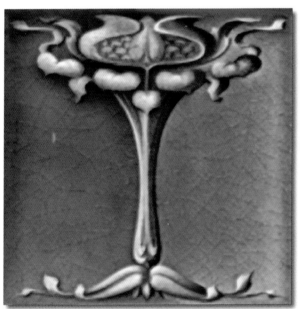

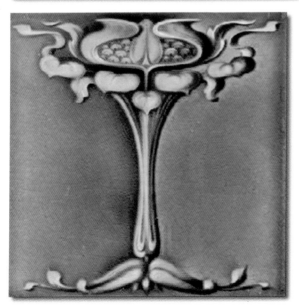

W. & E. Corn Brothers

W. & E. Corn Brothers located in Longport, Staffordshire started producing tiles in 1891. About 1895 they changed their name to Corn Brothers and continued to produce quality tiles until 1904. Corn Brothers were major manufacturers of tile, especially Art Nouveau.

Ultimate Art Nouveau designed tile by Corn Bros. Very good condition. $125-$150.

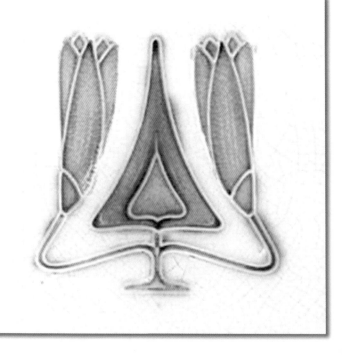

All of these tiles were done by Corn Brothers. They measure 6". They are in very good condition. $100-$125.

All of these tiles were done by Corn Brothers. They measure 6". They are in very good condition. $100-$125.

29

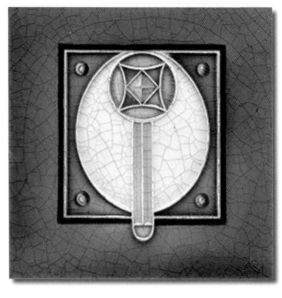

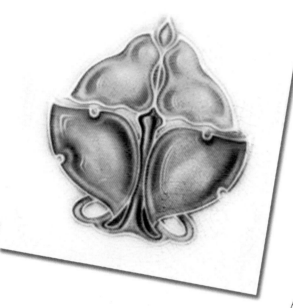

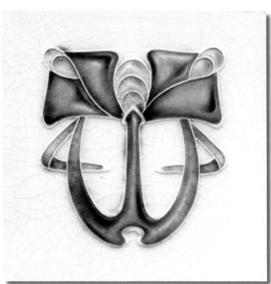

All of these tiles were done by Corn Brothers.
They measure 6". They are in very good condition.
$100-$125.

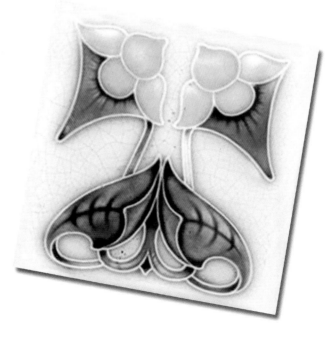

All of these tiles were done by Corn Brothers. They measure 6". They are in very good condition. $100-$125.

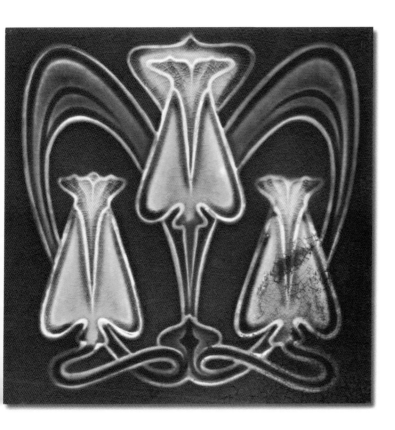

All of these tiles were done by Corn Brothers. They measure 6". They are in very good condition. $85-$100.

All of these tiles were done by Corn Brothers. They measure 6". They are in very good condition. $85-$100.

Craven Dunnill & Company

Craven Dunnill & Company was located in
Jackfield, Shropshire c1871-1910.

These two tiles with a peacock
feather design were done by Craven
Dunnill. Both are 6" and in very good
condition. $100-$135.

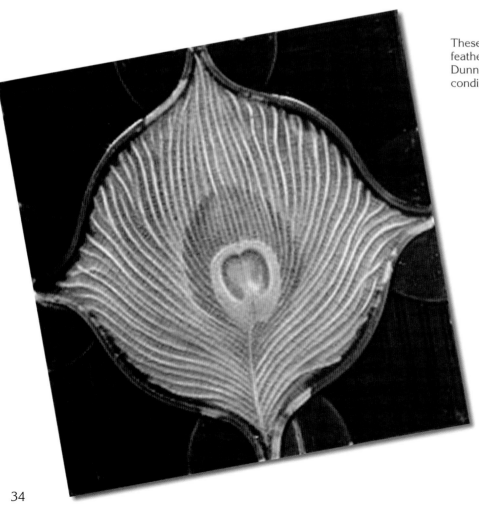

Doulton & Company, Ltd.

Doulton & Company, Ltd., was located in Lambeth, London c1880-1900.

Hand painted tile done by Doulton & Company. Artist initials on the reverse, E.M. Very good condition. This is a 6" tile. $150.

Two press molded designs done by Doulton & Company, same design different glazes. This is a 6" tile in very good condition. $100-$125.

Extremely good Art Nouveau designed tile by Doulton & Company. Doulton tiles are extremely rare. This is a 6" tile in fine condition. $150-$200.

Gibbons Hinton & Company

Gibbons Hinton & Company was located at Brierley Hill, Staffordshire c1895-1910.

These tiles were done by Gibbons Hinton & Company. They are 6" tiles and in very good condition. $100-$125

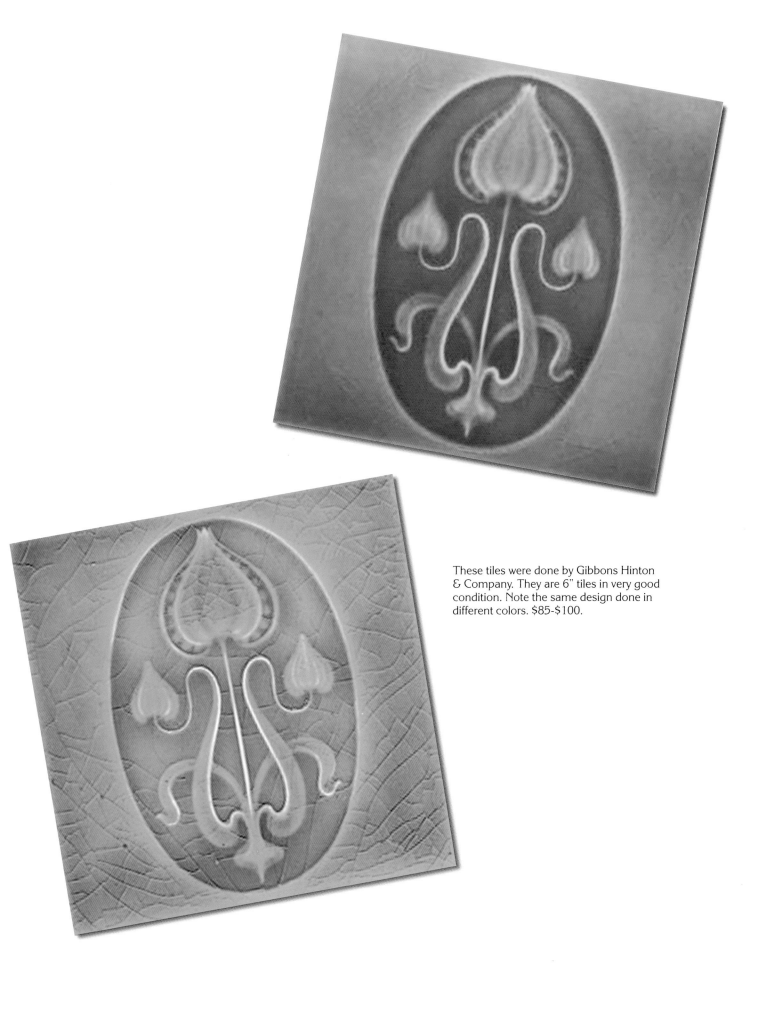

These tiles were done by Gibbons Hinton & Company. They are 6" tiles in very good condition. Note the same design done in different colors. $85-$100.

Godwin & Hewitt; Godwin & Thynne

Godwin & Hewitt located in Hereford c1882-1900.

Godwin & Thynne was located in Hereford c1909-1925.

These tiles were done by Godwin Hewitt. They are 6" tiles in very good condition. $100-$135.

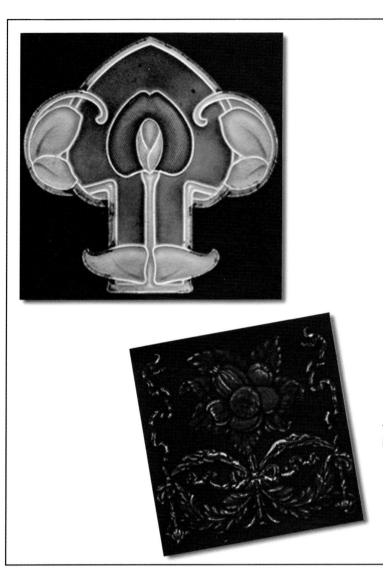

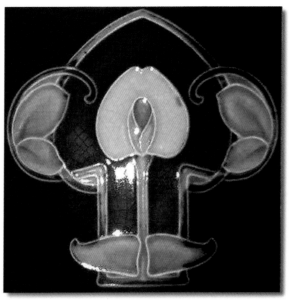

These tiles were done by Godwin Hewitt. They are 6" tiles in very good condition. $100-$135.

This tile was done by Godwin & Thynne. It is a 6"tile in good condition. $100.

H. & R. Johnson, Ltd.

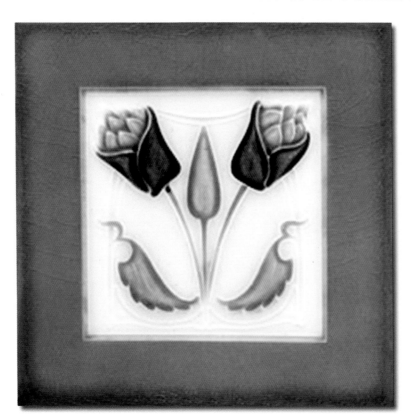

H. & R. Johnson, Ltd., was located in Cobridge, Staffordshire c1901-1930. They did some wonderful Art Nouveau designs within this time frame. H. & R. Johnson merged with H. Richards around 1968.

These are all 6" tiles done by H. & R. Johnson. They are in very good condition. $100-$125.

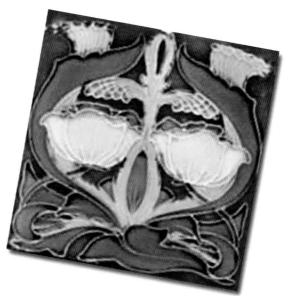

These are all 6" tiles done by H. & R. Johnson. They are in very good condition. $100-$125.

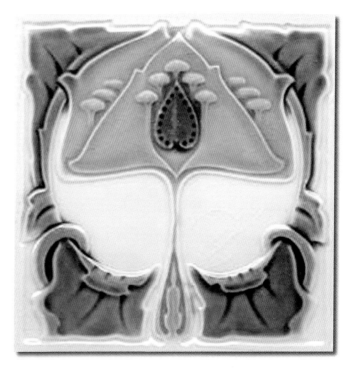

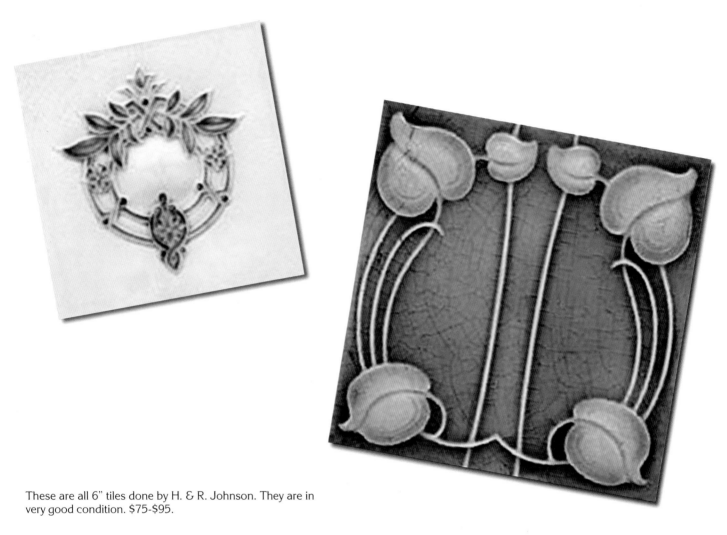

These are all 6" tiles done by H. & R. Johnson. They are in very good condition. $75-$95.

Lee & Boulton

Lee & Boulton was located in Tunstall,Staffordshire c1896-1902.

These tiles were done by Lee & Boulton. They are all 6" tiles in good condition. Note same design in different colors. $100-$135.

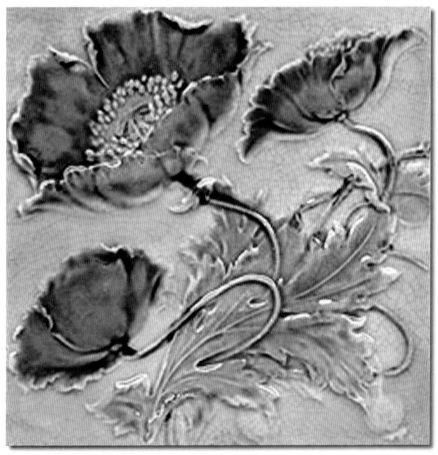

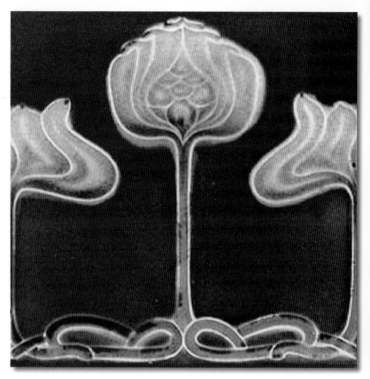

These tiles were done by Lee & Boulton. They are all 6" tiles in good condition. Note same design in different colors. $100-$135.

Tiles done by Lee & Boulton. Note how they were made to run together.

Malkin Edge & Company

Malkin Edge & Company manufactured tiles from c1870-1900. They were located in Burslem, Staffordshire.

Tiles were all done by Malkin Edge & Company. They are all 6" tiles and in very good condition. $100-$125.

Tiles were all done by Malkin Edge & Company. They are all 6" tiles and in very good condition. $100-$125.

Marsden Tile Company; Maw & Company

Marsden Tile Company was located in Burslem, Staffordshire c1880-1918.

Maw & Company was located in Broseley, Shropshire until 1883 and then moved to Jackfield, Shropshire c1883-1930, the company continued in business until almost 1969. They actually did some reproduction Art Nouveau in the late 1960s.

This tile design has been seen on Marsden Tile Company backs as well as Josiah Wedgwood & Sons. The condition is very good. $100-$125.

This tile was done by Maw & Company. $100-$125.

Alfred Meakin & Company

Alfred Meakin & Company, c1895-1910.

These tiles were done by Alfred Meakin &
Company. They are all 6" tiles in very good
condition.$100-$135.

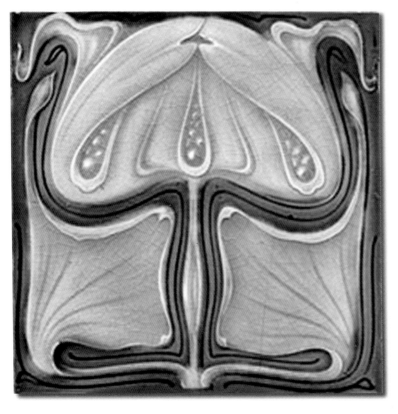

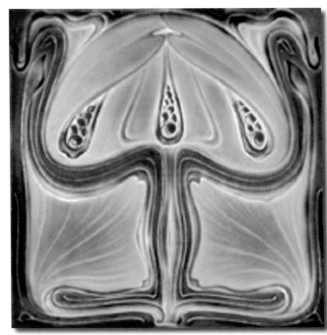

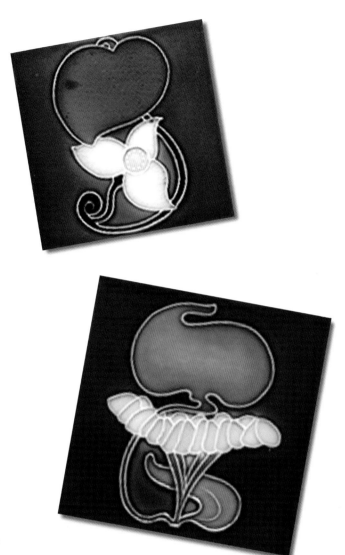

These tiles were done by Alfred Meakin &
Company. They are all 6" tiles in very good
condition.$100-$135.

These tiles were done by Alfred Meakin & Company. They are all 6" tiles in very good condition. $75-95.

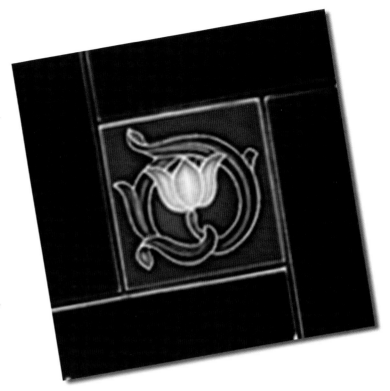

These tiles were done by Alfred Meakin & Company. They are all 6" tiles in very good condition. $45-$65.

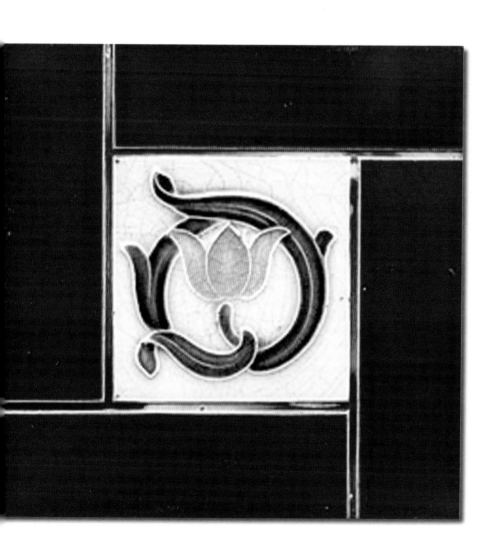

Mintons China Works

Mintons China Works, c1868-1910. Located in Stoke-on-Trent, Staffordshire. Minton was one of the major tile manufacturers of all time and the dominant tile producer of the 1870s. They produced numerous designs and series tiles, as well as fine handpainted and artist decorated tiles.

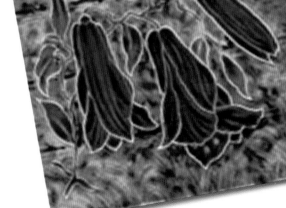

These tiles were done by Mintons China Works. They are all 6" tiles. $125-$145.

These tiles were done by Mintons China Works. They are all 6" tiles. $75-$100.

Minton, Hollins & Company

Minton, Hollins & Company, c1875-1930. They were located in Stoke-on-Trent, Staffordshire. Most Art Nouveau tiles that they produced date c1895-1900.

This whimsical tile is done by Minton Hollins & Company. It is a 6" tile. $150.

These tiles were all done by Minton Hollins & Company. They measure 6" and are in very good condition. $100-$135.

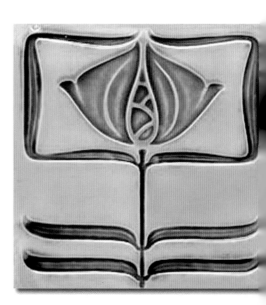

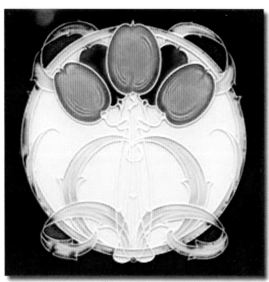

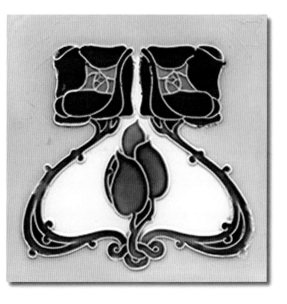

These tiles were all done by Minton Hollins & Company. They measure 6" and are in very good condition. $100-$135.

These tiles were all done by Minton Hollins & Company. They measure 6" and are in very good condition. $75-$100.

H.A. Ollivant

H.A. Ollivant, manufactured tiles from 1890-1908. They were located in Stoke-on-Trent, Staffordshire. They produced many good quality tile designs including Art Nouveau.

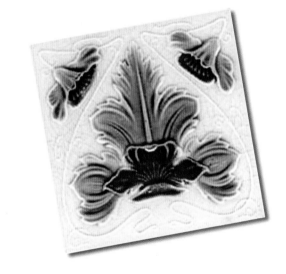

These tiles were all done by H.A. Ollivant. They are all 6" tiles in fine condition. Note the same design done in different color combinations. $100-$135.

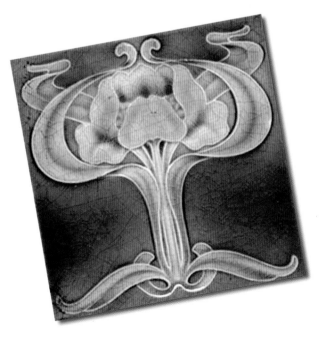

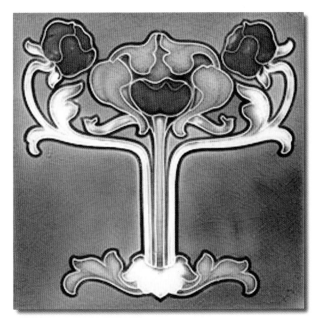

These tiles were all done by H.A. Ollivant. They are all 6"
tiles in fine condition. Note the same design done in
different color combinations. $100-$135.

Pilkingtons Tile & Pottery Company, Ltd.

Pilkingtons Tile & Pottery Company Ltd. was started in 1892. They were located at Clifton Junction, Manchester. They were extremely successful in the Art Nouveau market c1892-1910. In part, their success was due to the noted designers they employed, C.F.A. Vorsey, Walter Crane and Lewis Day. Pilkingtons produced some of the finest Art Nouveau tiles and acquired supremacy in the world of tile manufacturing in a very short period of time. They continued to produce fine quality tiles into the 20th century.

These tiles were done by Pilkingtons Tile & Pottery Company, Ltd. They are all 6" tiles in good condition. Note same design in different color combinations. $100-$125.

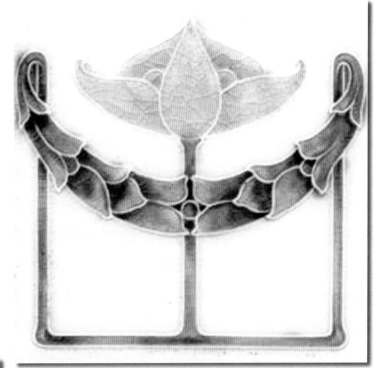

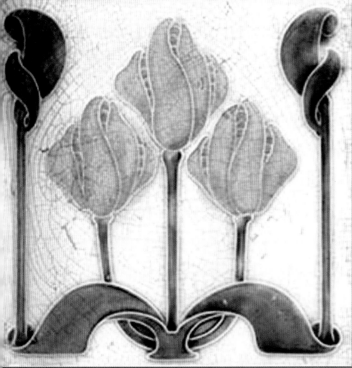

These tiles were done by Pilkingtons Tile & Pottery Company, Ltd. They are all 6" tiles in good condition. $100-$125.

These tiles were done by Pilkingtons Tile & Pottery Company, Ltd. They are all 6" tiles in good condition. $100-$125.

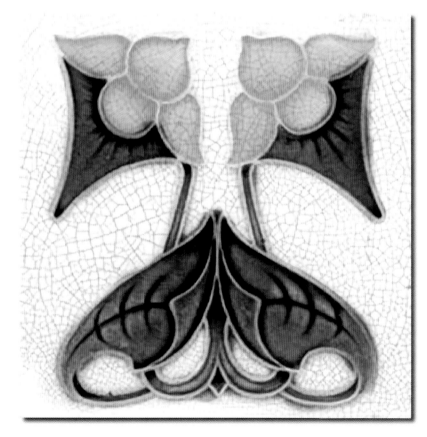

These tiles were done by Pilkingtons Tile & Pottery Company, Ltd. They are all 6" tiles in good condition. These designs are attributed to Lewis Day. $100-$125.

These tiles were done by Pilkingtons Tile & Pottery Company, Ltd. They are all 6" tiles in good condition. Note same design in different color combinations. $125-$150.

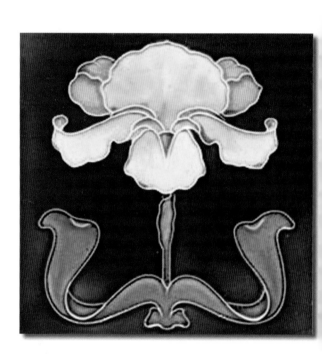

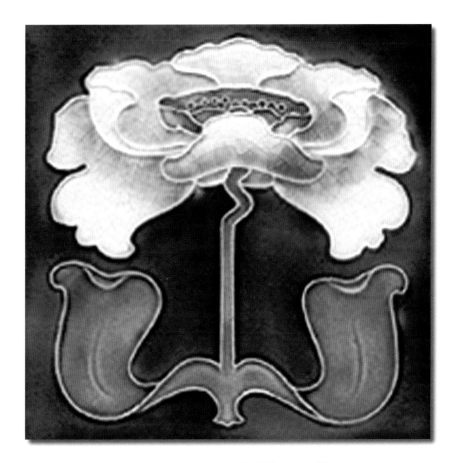

This tile was done by Pilkingtons Tile
& Pottery Company, Ltd. It is a
wonderful 6" design. $125-$150.

These tiles were done by Pilkingtons Tile & Pottery Company, Ltd. They are all 6" tiles in good condition. Note same design in different color combinations. $75-$100.

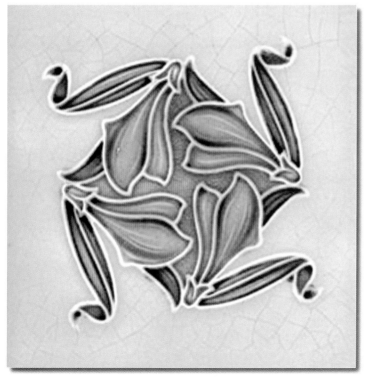

These tiles were done by Pilkingtons Tile & Pottery Company, Ltd. They are all 6" tiles in good condition. $100-$150.

We believe this tile was done by Pilkingtons Tile & Pottery Company, Ltd. It was the bottom tile from a larger vertical panel. A great design $100-$125.

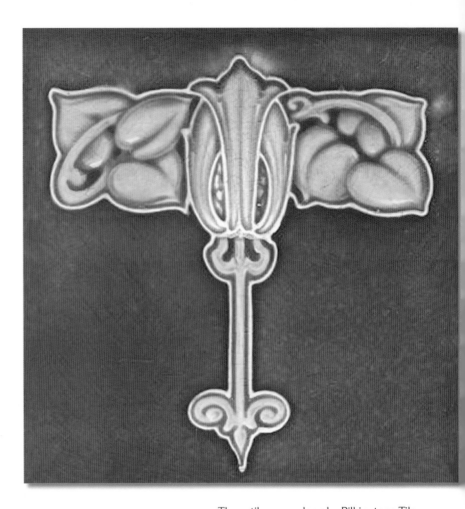

These tiles were done by Pilkingtons Tile & Pottery Company, Ltd. They are 6" tiles in good condition. These two tiles date later than the rest shown, about 1930. $75-$100.

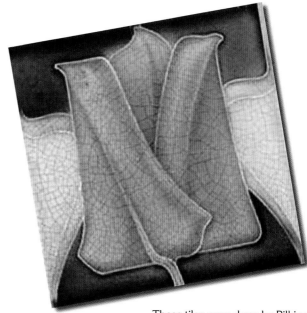

These tiles were done by Pilkingtons Tile & Pottery Company, Ltd. They are 6" tiles in good condition. These two tiles are attributed to C.F.A. Vorsey. Note how they ran together in a horizontal run. $100-$135.

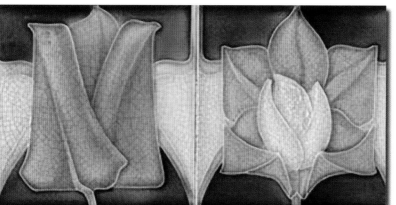

These tiles were done by Pilkingtons Tile & Pottery Company, Ltd. They are 6" tiles in good condition. These two tiles are attributed to C.F.A. Vorsey. Note how they ran together in a vertical panel. $250-$300.

Rhodes Tile Company

Rhodes Tile Company was located in Tunstall, Staffordshire c1902-1906. They produced many Art Nouveau wall tiles.

These two tiles were done by Rhodes Tile Company. They are 6" tiles in good condition. $100-$125.

H. Richards Tile Company

H. Richards Tile Company was formed in 1902 and continued making tiles into the 1930s. They were located in Staffordshire. They produced some extremely pretty Art Nouveau designs for their tiles. They merged with H. & R. Johnson around 1968.

This is a very impressive 6" tile done by a H. Richards Tile Company. The human form on Art Nouveau tiles is very rare and will command a higher price than the floral, or abstract motif.

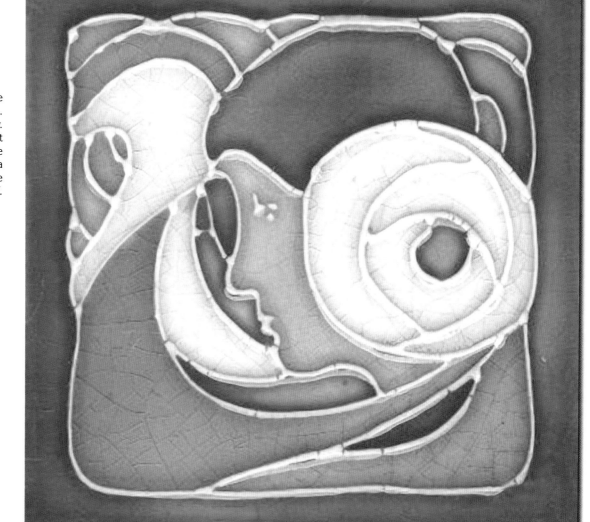

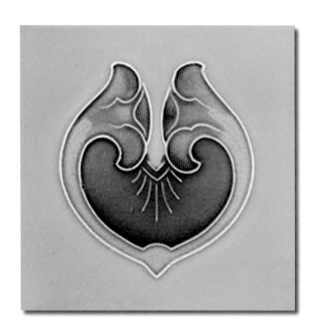

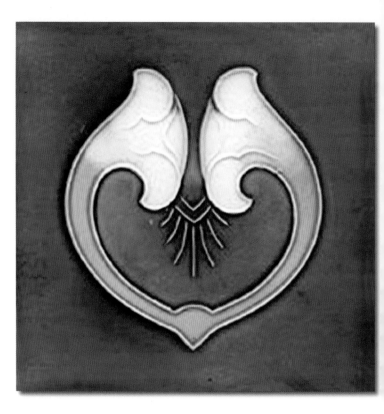

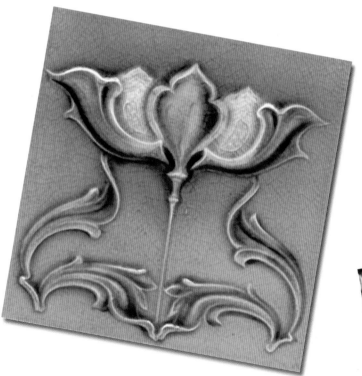

These tiles are done by H. Richards Tile Company. They are 6" tiles in very good condition. $100-$125.

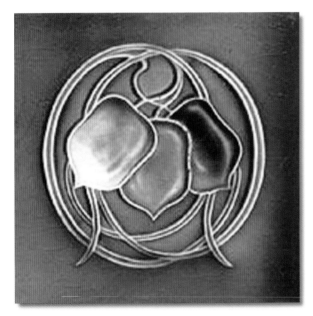

These tiles are done by H. Richards Tile Company. They are 6" tiles in very good condition. $100-$125

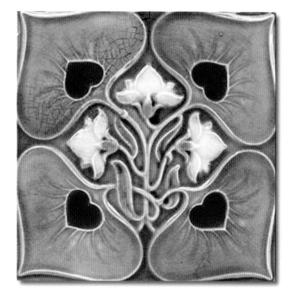

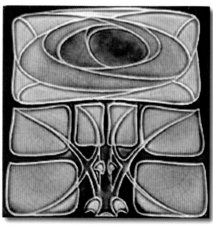

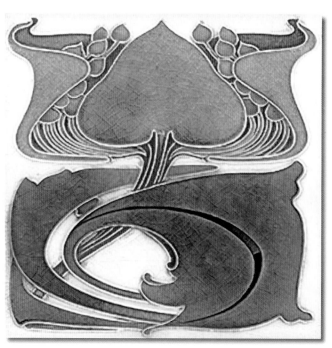

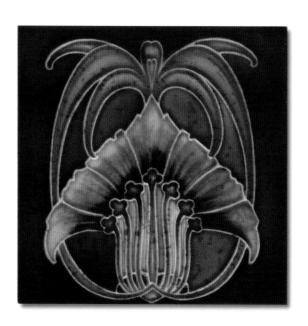

These tiles are done by H. Richards Tile Company.
They are 6" tiles in very good condition. $120-$150.

These tiles are done by H. Richards Tile Company. They are 6" tiles in very good condition. $120-$150.

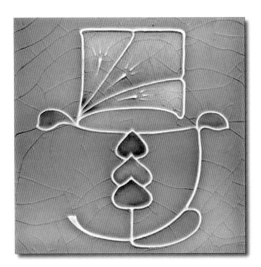

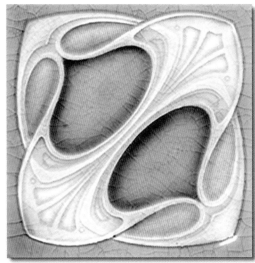

These tiles are done by H. Richards Tile Company. They are 6" tiles in very good condition. $120-$150.

These tiles are done by H. Richards Tile Company. They are 6" tiles in very good condition. Note the same design in different colors. Multi-color $125. Solid colors $85 -$100.

These tiles are done by H. Richards Tile Company. They are 6" tiles in very good condition. Note the same tile in different color combinations. $100-$135.

76

These tiles are done by H. Richards Tile Company. They are 6" tiles in very good condition. $100-$135.

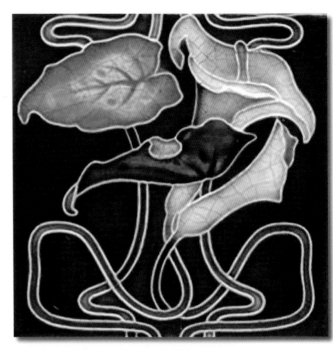

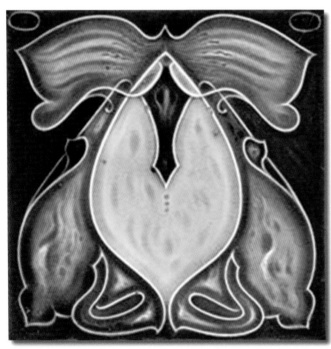

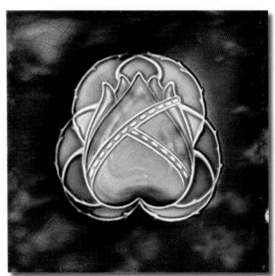

These tiles are done by H. Richards Tile Company. They are 6" tiles in very good condition. $100-$135.

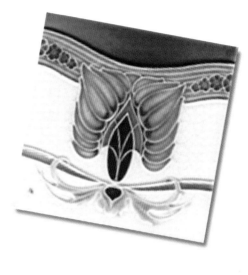

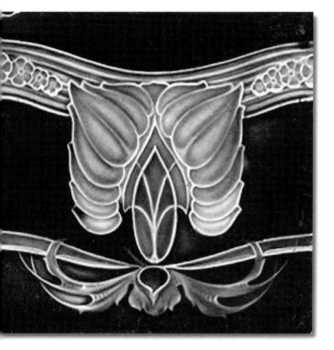

These tiles are done by H. Richards Tile Company. They are 6" tiles in very good condition. Note the different color combinations on the same design. $100-$135.

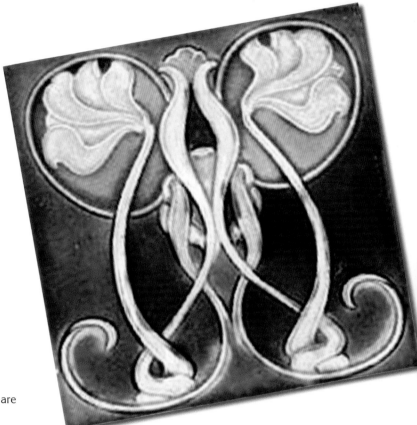

These tiles are done by H. Richards Tile Company. They are 6" tiles in very good condition. Note the different color combinations on the same design. $100-$135.

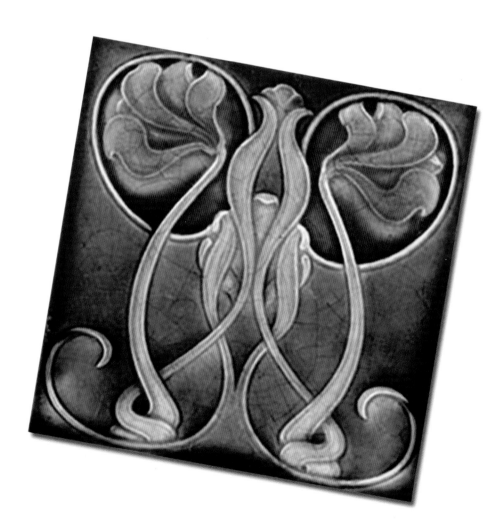

These tiles are done by H. Richards Tile Company. They are 6" tiles in very good condition. Note three different color combinations. $85-$100.

These tiles are done by H. Richards Tile Company. They are 6" tiles in very good condition. $75-$100.

These tiles are done by H. Richards Tile Company. They are 6" tiles in very good condition. $75-$100.

Sherwin & Cotton

Sherwin & Cotton, manufactured tiles from 1877-1911. They were located in Hanley, Staffordshire. This company had a good reputation for producing very high quality tiles. They produced some fine examples of Art Nouveau tiles with wonderful rich glazes.

These tiles were all done by Sherwin & Cotton. They are all 6" tiles in good condion. $120-$150.

These tiles were all done by Sherwin & Cotton. They are all 6" tiles in good condion. $120-$150.

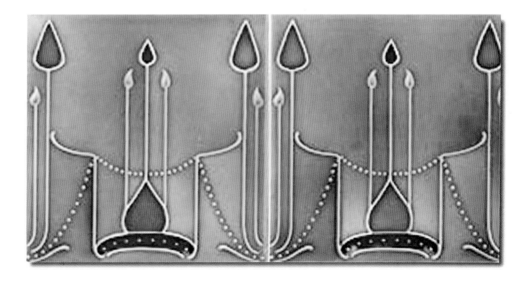

These tiles were all done by Sherwin &
Cotton. They are all 6" tiles in good
condion. $120-$150.

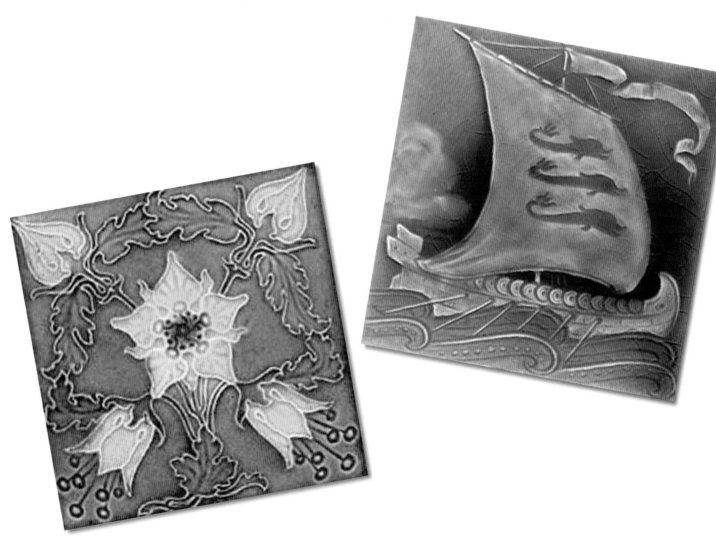

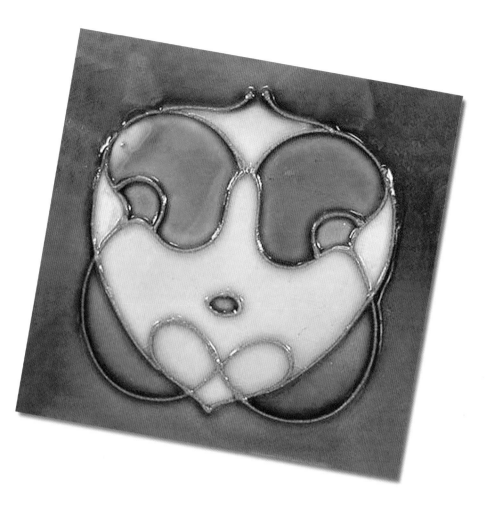

These tiles were all done by Sherwin & Cotton. They are all 6" tiles in good condion. $120-$150.

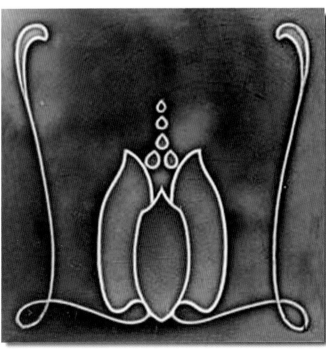

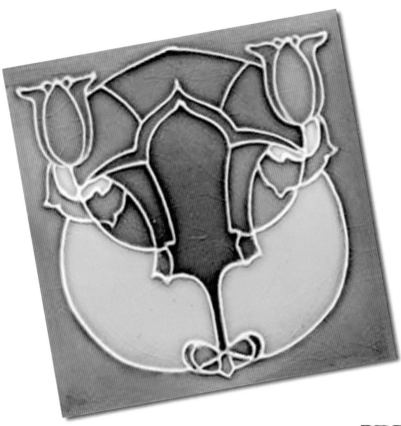

These tiles were all done by Sherwin & Cotton. They are all 6" tiles in good condion. $120-$150.

This tile was done by Sherwin & Cotton. Note broken corner. $50-$65 in this condition. It is a 6" tile.

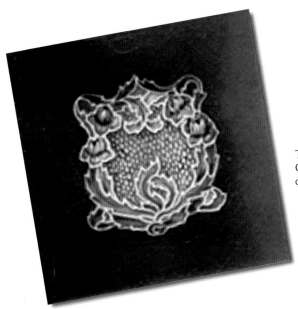

This tile was done by Sherwin & Cotton. It is a 6" tile in good condition $85.

These tiles were done by Sherwin & Cotton. They are two 6" tiles that make up a vertical panel. Good condition. $250-$300.

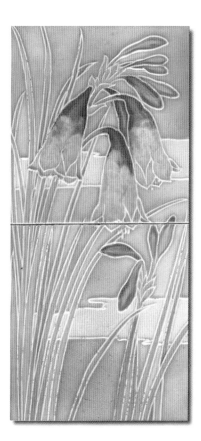

Miscellaneous Tile Companies

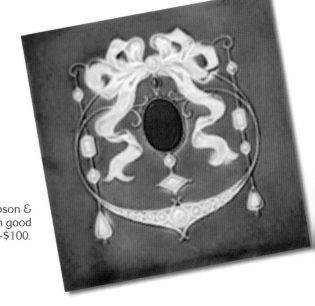

T. A. Simpson & Company, Ltd was located in Burslem, Staffordshire c1895-1890.

Stubbs & Hodgart was located in Longport, Staffordshire c1890-1900. This company made a fine contribution to Art Nouveau tiles.

This tile was done by T.A. Simpson & Company. It is a 6" tile in good condition. $85-$100.

Josiah Wedgwood & Sons Ltd, were in business from 1761. Tile production was from c1870-1900. They were located in Etruria, Staffordshire. It is unusual to see Art Nouveau tiles from this company who were famous for their transfer printed tiles. They discontinued tile production in 1902.

George Wooliscroft & Sons, Ltd. Art Nouveau tiles were made by this company c1900. They started in Chesterton, Staffordshire around 1850 and produced a full range of designs. The quality of their Art Nouveau tile designs was absolutely superb as well as their glazing.

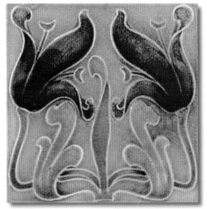

These tiles were done by Stubbs & Hodgart. They are 6" tiles in good condition. $100-$135.

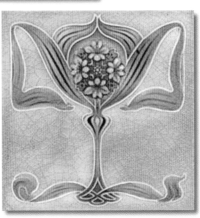

These tiles were done by Josiah Wedgwood & Sons, Ltd. They are 6" tiles in good condition. $100-$125.

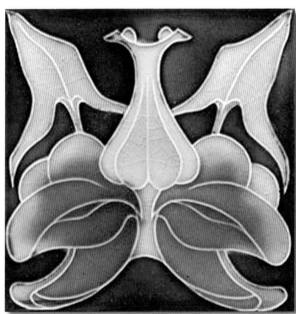

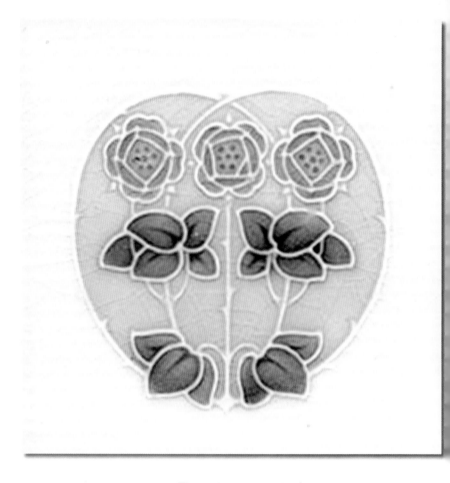

These tiles are done by George Wooliscroft & Sons, Ltd. They are 6" tiles, all in good condition. $100-$135.

Unattributed Tile Manufacturers

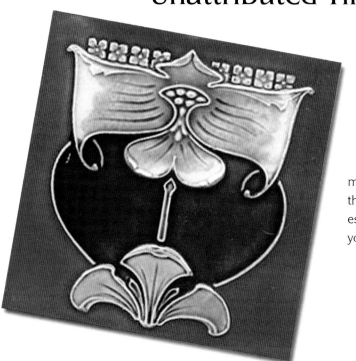

In this section you will see some really amazing tile designs by many different tile companies working in the time frame. We find the different color applications on the same tile design very interesting and hope you will as well. This part of the book will also show you an incredible assortment of designs and color schemes.

These are all 6" tiles. They are done by various manufacturers. We will not attribute these designs to any one specific company. They are all wonderful Art Nouveau designs. Please note the same design done in many different color combinations. $100 -$150.

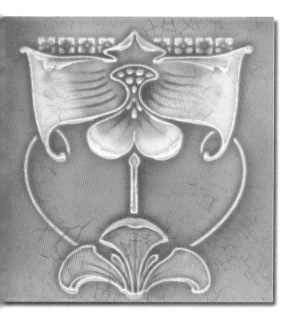

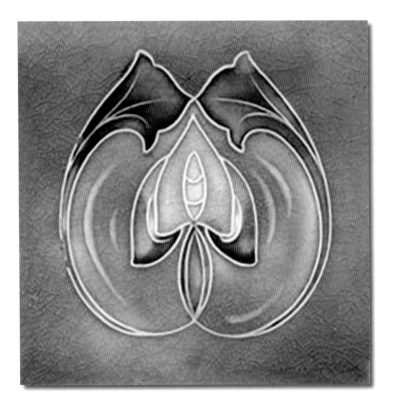

These are all 6" tiles. They are done by various manufacturers. We will not attribute these designs to any one specific company. They are all wonderful Art Nouveau designs. Please note the same design done in many different color combinations. $100 -$150.

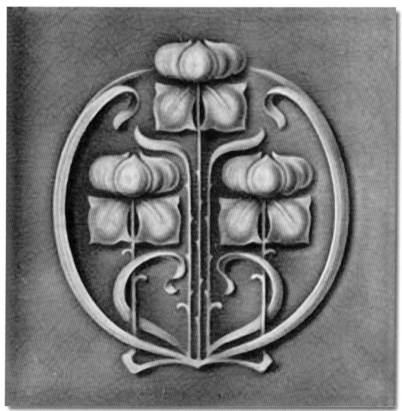

These are all 6" tiles. They are done by various manufacturers. We will not attribute these designs to any one specific company. They are all wonderful Art Nouveau designs. Please note the same design done in many different color combinations. $100 -$150.

These are all 6" tiles. They are done by various manufacturers. We will not attribute these designs to any one specific company. They are all wonderful Art Nouveau designs. Please note the same design done in many different color combinations. $100 -$150.

These are all 6" tiles. They are done by various manufacturers. We will not attribute these designs to any one specific company. They are all wonderful Art Nouveau designs. Please note the same design done in many different color combinations. $100 -$150.

These are all 6" tiles. They are done by various manufacturers. We will not attribute these designs to any one specific company. They are all wonderful Art Nouveau designs. Please note the same design done in many different color combinations. $100 -$150.

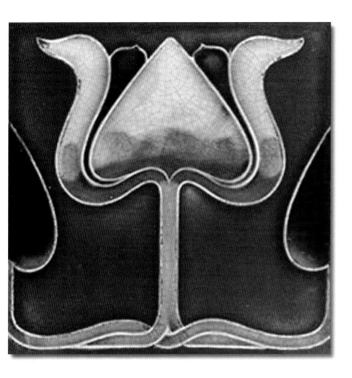

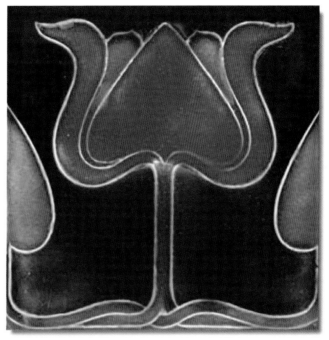

These are all 6" tiles. They are done by various manufacturers. We will not attribute these designs to any one specific company. They are all wonderful Art Nouveau designs. Please note the same design done in many different color combinations. $100 -$150.

These are all 6" tiles. They are done by various manufacturers. We will not attribute these designs to any one specific company. They are all wonderful Art Nouveau designs. Please note the same design done in many different color combinations. $100 -$150.

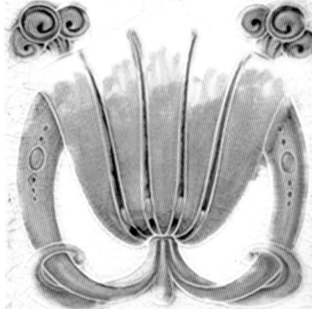

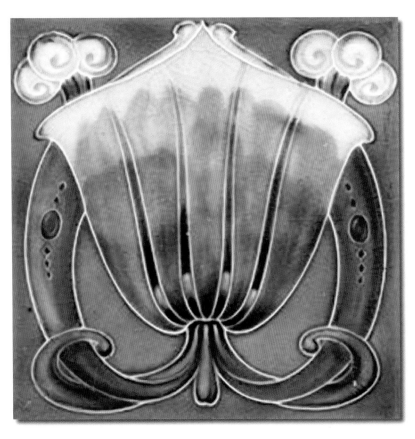

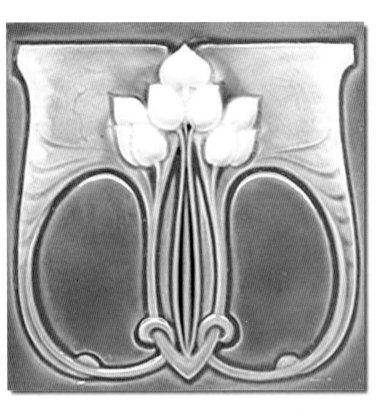

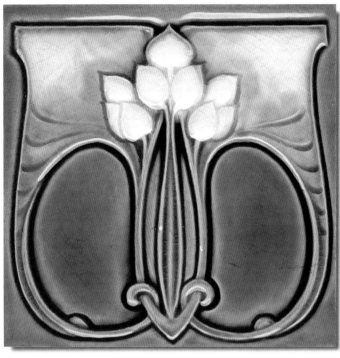

These are all 6" tiles. They are done by various manufacturers. We will not attribute these designs to any one specific company. They are all wonderful Art Nouveau designs. Please note the same design done in many different color combinations. $100 -$150.

These are all 6" tiles. They are done by various manufacturers. We will not attribute these designs to any one specific company. They are all wonderful Art Nouveau designs. Please note the same design done in many different color combinations. $100 -$150.

These are all 6" tiles. They are done by various manufacturers. We will not attribute these designs to any one specific company. They are all wonderful Art Nouveau designs. Please note the same design done in many different color combinations. $100 -$150.

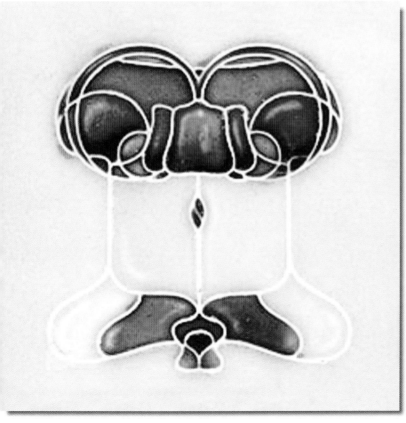

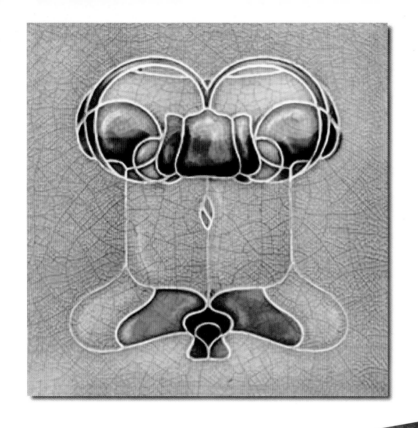

These are all 6" tiles. They are done by various manufacturers. We will not attribute these designs to any one specific company. They are all wonderful Art Nouveau designs. Please note the same design done in many different color combinations. $100 -$150.

These are all 6" tiles. They are done by various
manufacturers. We will not attribute these designs to any
one specific company. They are all wonderful Art Nouveau
designs. Please note the same design done in many
different color combinations. $100 -$150.

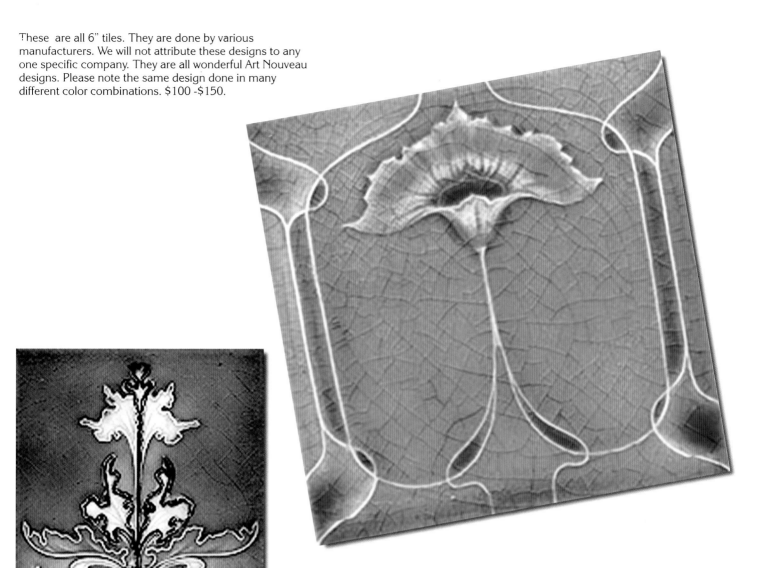

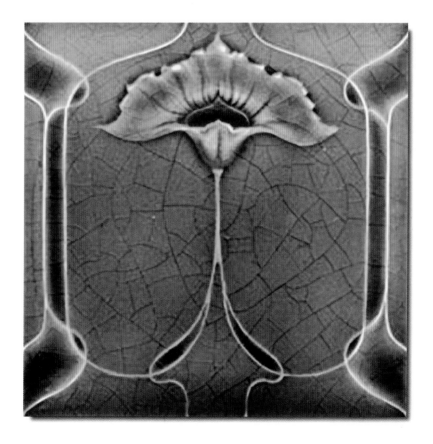

These are all 6" tiles. They are done by various manufacturers. We will not attribute these designs to any one specific company. They are all wonderful Art Nouveau designs. Please note the same design done in many different color combinations. $100 -$150.

These are all 6" tiles. They are done by various manufacturers. We will not attribute these designs to any one specific company. They are all wonderful Art Nouveau designs. Please note the same design done in many different color combinations. $100 -$150.

These are all 6" tiles. They are done by various manufacturers. We will not attribute these designs to any one specific company. They are all wonderful Art Nouveau designs. Please note the same design done in many different color combinations. $100 -$150.

These are all 6" tiles. They are done by various manufacturers. We will not attribute these designs to any one specific company. They are all wonderful Art Nouveau designs. Please note the same design done in many different color combinations. $100 -$150.

These are all 6" tiles. They are done by various manufacturers. We will not attribute these designs to any one specific company. They are all wonderful Art Nouveau designs. Please note the same design done in many different color combinations. $100 -$150.

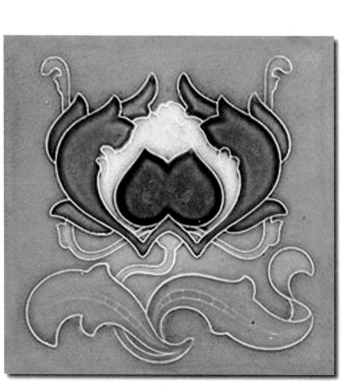

These are all 6" tiles. They are done by various manufacturers that we will not attribute to any one specific company. They are all wonderful Art Nouveau designs. $100 -$125.

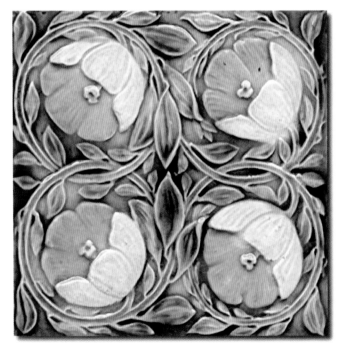

These are all 6" tiles. They are done by various manufacturers that we will not attribute to any one specific company. They are all wonderful Art Nouveau designs. $100 -$125.

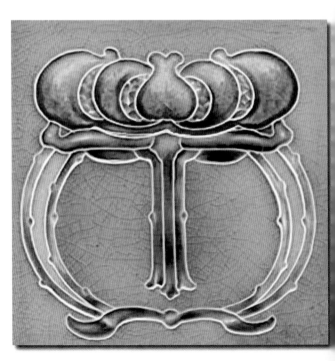

These are all 6" tiles. They are done by various manufacturers that we will not attribute to any one specific company. They are all wonderful Art Nouveau designs. $100 -$125.

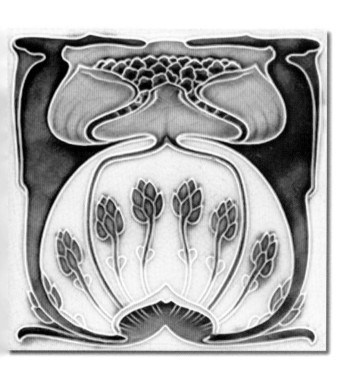

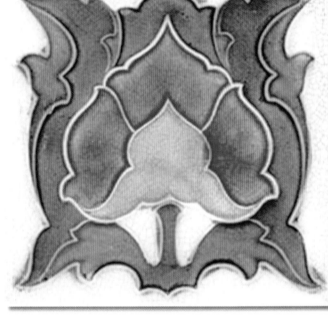

These are all 6" tiles. They are done by various manufacturers that we will not attribute to any one specific company. They are all wonderful Art Nouveau designs. $100 -$125.

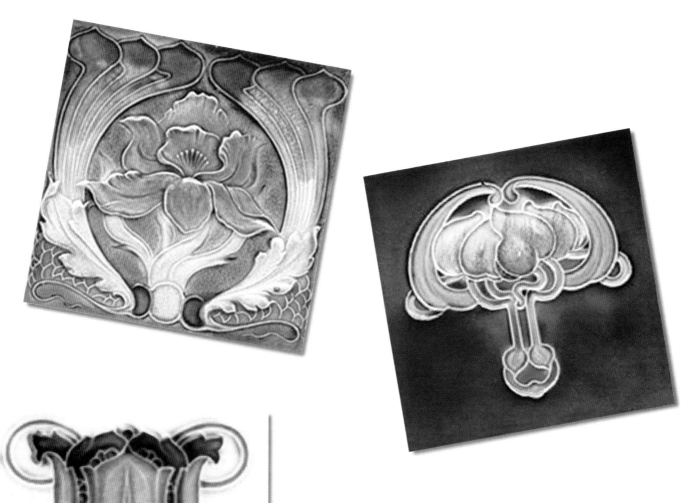

These are all 6" tiles. They are done by various manufacturers that we will not attribute to any one specific company. They are all wonderful Art Nouveau designs. $100 -$125.

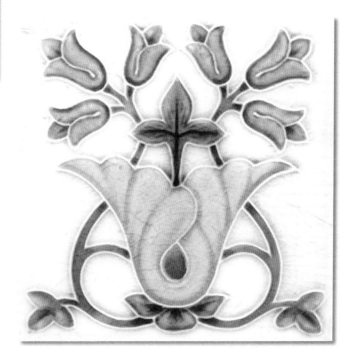

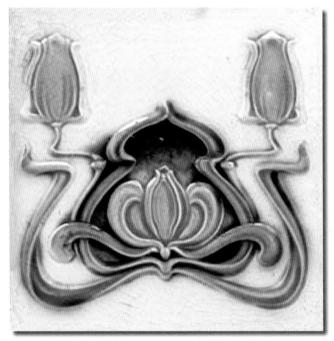

These are all 6" tiles. They are done by various manufacturers that we will not attribute to any one specific company. They are all wonderful Art Nouveau designs. $100 -$125.

These are all 6" tiles. They are done by various manufacturers that we will not attribute to any one specific company. They are all wonderful Art Nouveau designs. $100 -$125.

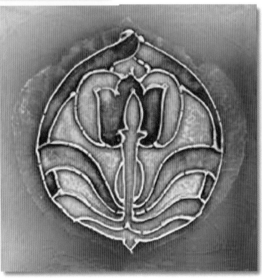

These are all 6" tiles. They are done by various manufacturers that we will not attribute to any one specific company. They are all wonderful Art Nouveau designs. $100 -$125.

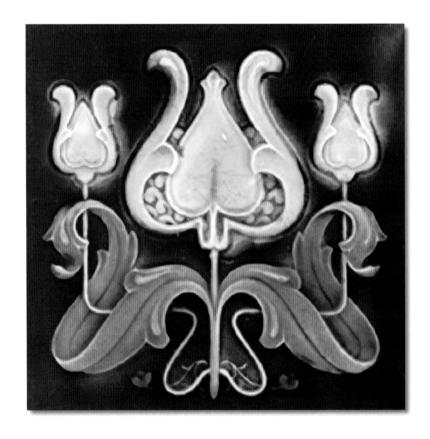

These are all 6" tiles. They are done by various manufacturers that we will not attribute to any one specific company. They are all wonderful Art Nouveau designs. $100 -$125.

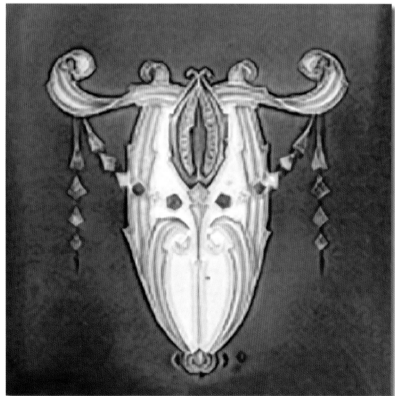

These are all 6" tiles. They are done by various manufacturers that we will not attribute to any one specific company. They are all wonderful Art Nouveau designs. $100 -$125.

120

These are all 6" tiles. They are done by various manufacturers that we will not attribute to any one specific company. They are all wonderful Art Nouveau designs. $100 -$125.

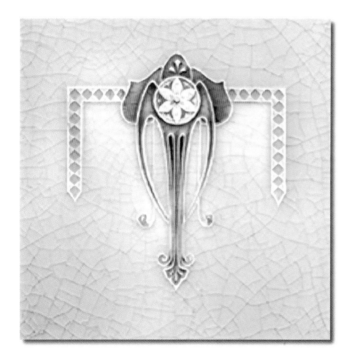

These are all 6" tiles. They are done by various manufacturers that we will not attribute to any one specific company. They are all wonderful Art Nouveau designs. $100 -$125.

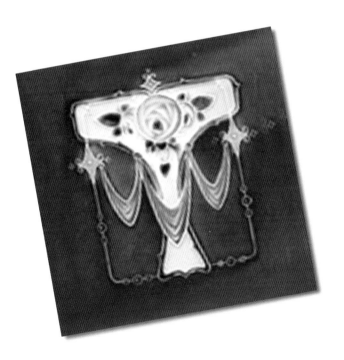

These are all 6" tiles. They are done by various manufacturers that we will not attribute to any one specific company. They are all wonderful Art Nouveau designs. $100 -$125.

These are all 6" tiles. They are done by various manufacturers that we will not attribute to any one specific company. They are all wonderful Art Nouveau designs. $100 -$125.

These are all 6" tiles. They are done by various manufacturers that we will not attribute to any one specific company. They are all wonderful Art Nouveau designs. $100 -$125.

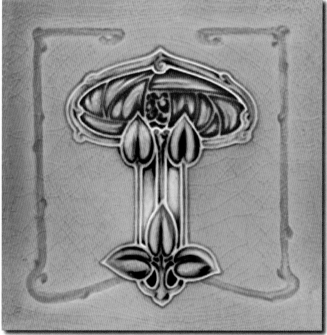

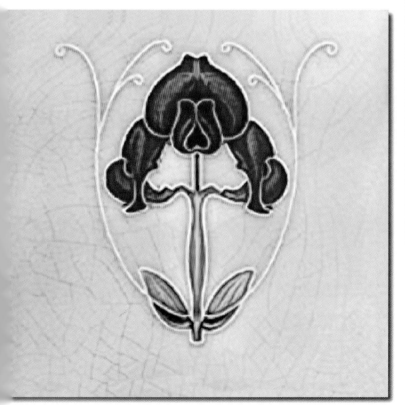

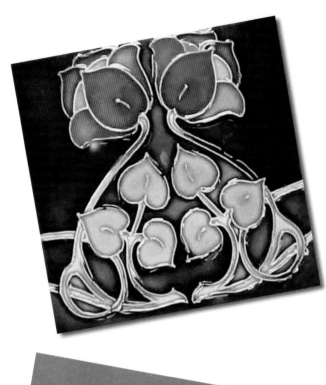

These are all 6" tiles. They are done by various manufacturers that we will not attribute to any one specific company. They are all wonderful Art Nouveau designs. $100 -$125.

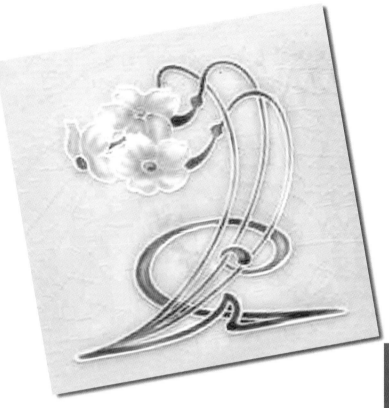

These are all 6" tiles. They are done by various manufacturers that we will not attribute to any one specific company. They are all wonderful Art Nouveau designs. $100 -$125.

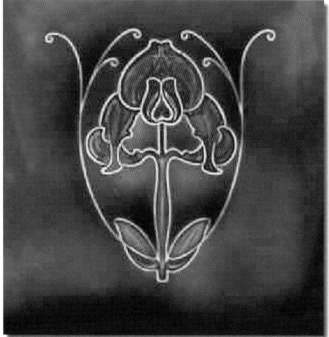

These are all 6" tiles. They are done by various manufacturers that we will not attribute to any one specific company. They are all wonderful Art Nouveau designs. $100 -$125.

These are all 6" tiles. They are done by various manufacturers that we will not attribute to any one specific company. They are all wonderful Art Nouveau designs. $100 -$125.

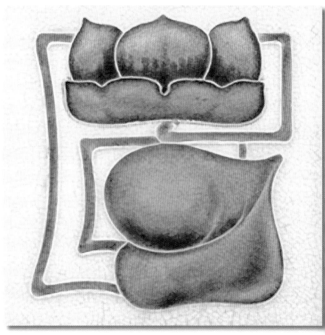

These are all 6" tiles. They are done by various manufacturers that we will not attribute to any one specific company. They are all wonderful Art Nouveau designs. $100 -$125.

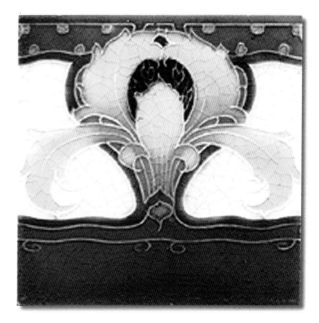

These are all 6" tiles. They are done by various manufacturers that we will not attribute to any one specific company. They are all wonderful Art Nouveau designs. $100 -$125.

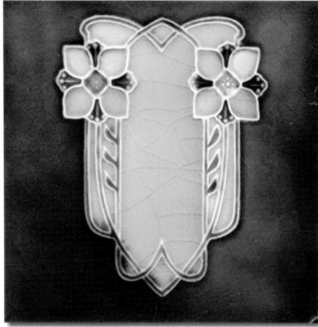

These are all 6" tiles. They are done by various manufacturers that we will not attribute to any one specific company. They are all wonderful Art Nouveau designs. $100 -$125.

These are all 6" tiles. They are done by various manufacturers that we will not attribute to any one specific company. They are all wonderful Art Nouveau designs. $100 -$125.

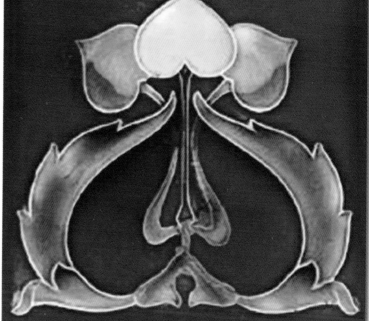

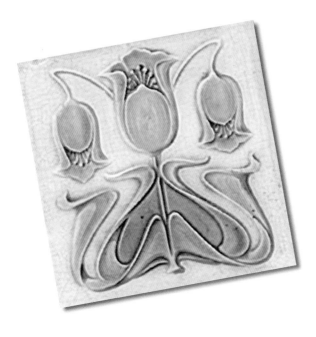

These are all 6" tiles. They are done by various manufacturers that we will not attribute to any one specific company. They are all wonderful Art Nouveau designs. $100 -$125.

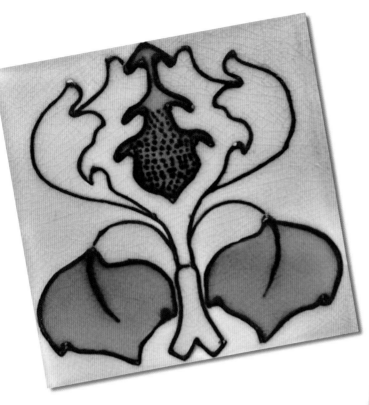

These are all 6" tiles. They are done by various manufacturers that we will not attribute to any one specific company. They are all wonderful Art Nouveau designs. $100 -$125.

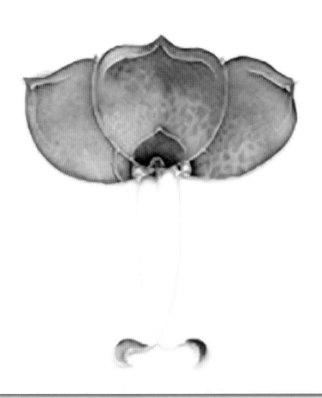

These are all 6" tiles. They are done by various manufacturers that we will not attribute to any one specific company. They are all wonderful Art Nouveau designs. $100 -$125.

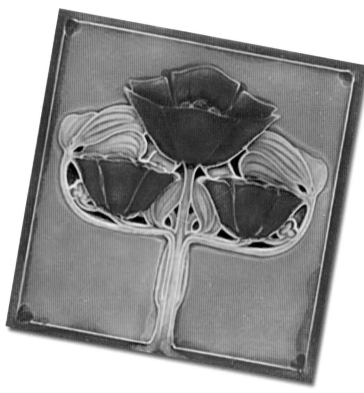

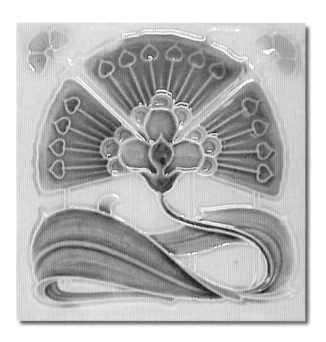

These are all 6" tiles. They are done by various manufacturers that we will not attribute to any one specific company. They are all wonderful Art Nouveau designs. $100 -$125.

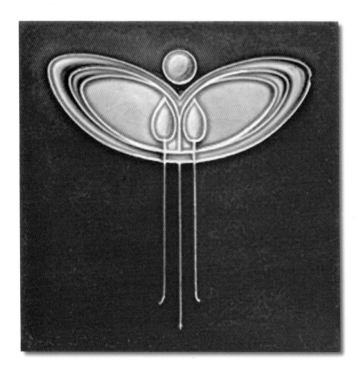

These are all 6" tiles. They are done by various manufacturers that we will not attribute to any one specific company. They are all wonderful Art Nouveau designs. $100 -$125.

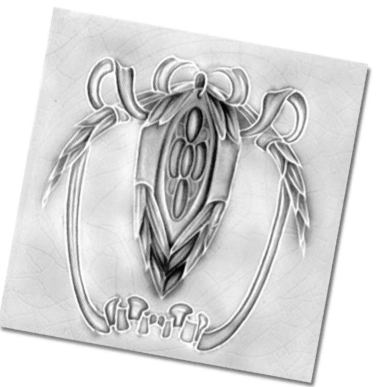

These are all 6" tiles. They are done by various manufacturers that we will not attribute to any one specific company. They are all wonderful Art Nouveau designs. $100 -$125.

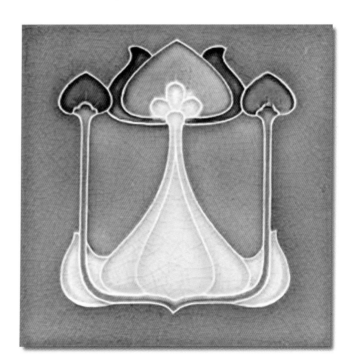

These are all 6" tiles. They are done by various manufacturers that we will not attribute to any one specific company. They are all wonderful Art Nouveau designs. $100 -$125.

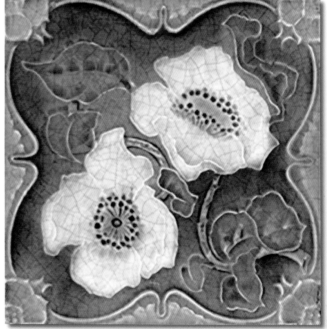

These are all 6" tiles. They are done by various manufacturers that we will not attribute to any one specific company. They are all wonderful Art Nouveau designs. $100 -$125.

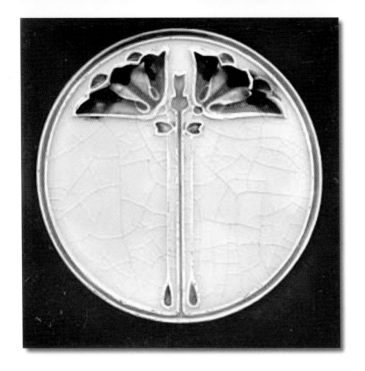

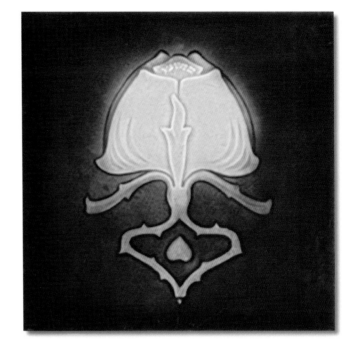

These are all 6" tiles. They are done by various manufacturers that we will not attribute to any one specific company. They are all wonderful Art Nouveau designs. $100 -$125.

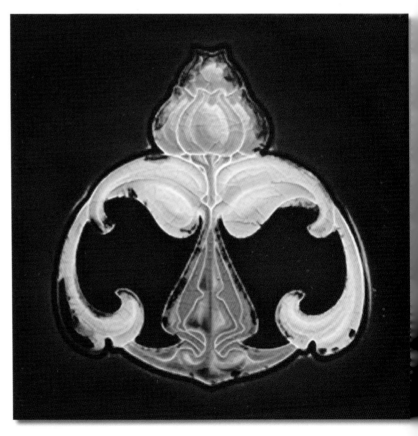

These are all 6" tiles. They are done by various manufacturers that we will not attribute to any one specific company. They are all wonderful Art Nouveau designs. $100 -$125.

These are all 6" tiles. They are done by various manufacturers that we will not attribute to any one specific company. They are all wonderful Art Nouveau designs. $100 -$125.

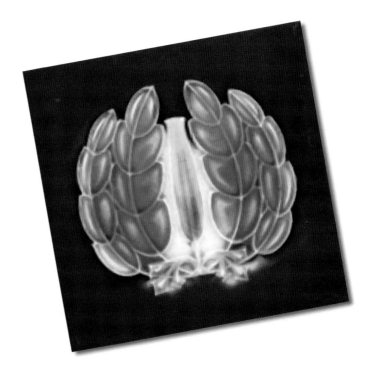

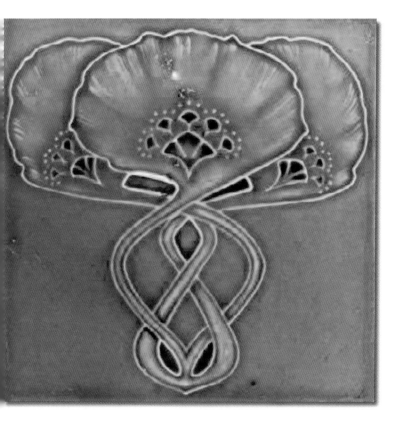

These are all 6" tiles. They are done by various manufacturers that we will not attribute to any one specific company. They are all wonderful Art Nouveau designs. $100 -$125.

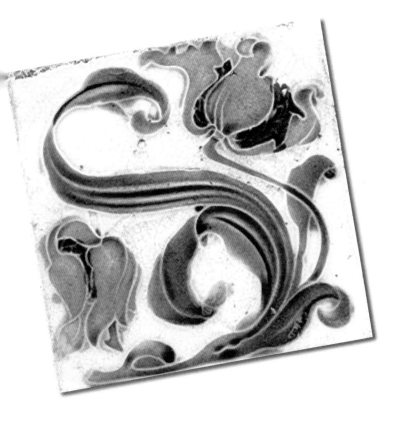

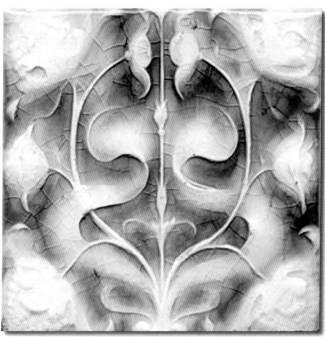

These are all 6" tiles. They are done by various manufacturers that we will not attribute to any one specific company. They are all wonderful Art Nouveau designs. $100 - $125.

146

These are all 6" tiles. They are done by various manufacturers that we will not attribute to any one specific company. They are all wonderful Art Nouveau designs. $100 -$125.

These are all 6" tiles. They are done by various manufacturers that we will not attribute to any one specific company. They are all wonderful Art Nouveau designs. $100 -$125.

These are all 6" tiles. They are done by various manufacturers that we will not attribute to any one specific company. They are all wonderful Art Nouveau designs. $100 -$125.

These are all 6" tiles. They are done by various manufacturers that we will not attribute to any one specific company. They are all wonderful Art Nouveau designs. $100 -$125.

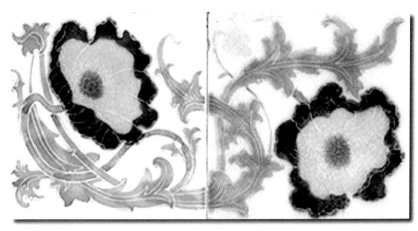

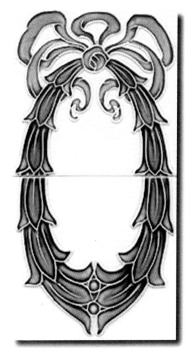

These are 6" tiles that make a two tile panel. These tiles are done by various manufacturers that we will not attribute to any one specific company. $150-$200.

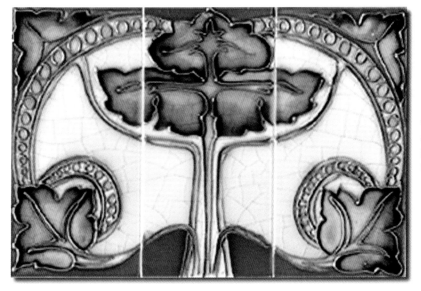

This is a wonderful panel done with three 3" x 6" tiles. It was part of a larger panel. Tile manufacturer unidentified. $200-$350.

This is a beautiful 8" tile that was placed in the top of a wood framed trivet. It is by an unidentified manufacturer. It is a classic Art Nouveau design with wonderful coloring. $225.

Four Square Designs

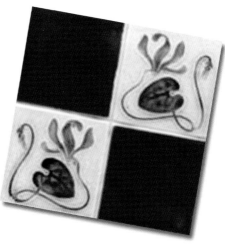

These are 6" tiles that are done in a four-square design having the design in only two corners of the tile. These tiles would have been used in installations or furniture backsplashes where they would have run together to make a pattern. These tiles are done by various manufacturers. $35-$65.

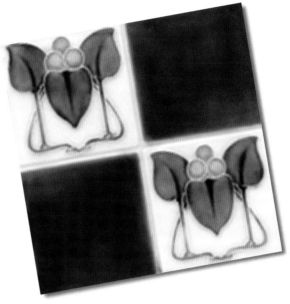

These are 6" tiles that are done in a four-square design having the design in only two corners of the tile. These tiles would have been used in installations or furniture backsplashes where they would have run together to make a pattern. These tiles are done by various manufacturers. $35-$65.

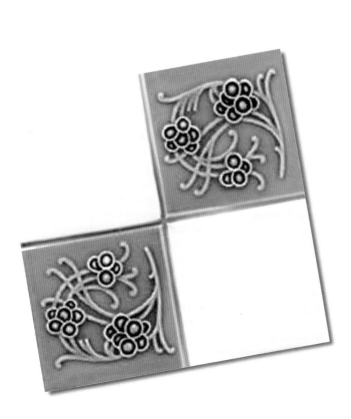

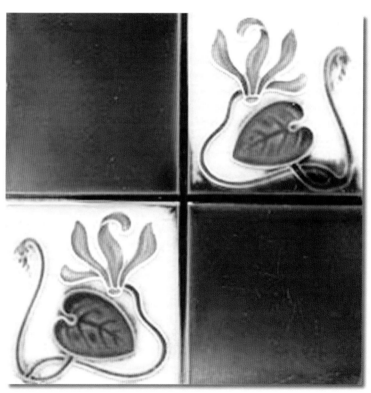

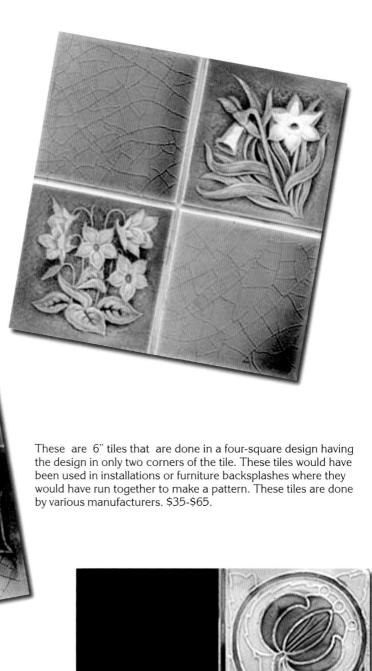

These are 6" tiles that are done in a four-square design having the design in only two corners of the tile. These tiles would have been used in installations or furniture backsplashes where they would have run together to make a pattern. These tiles are done by various manufacturers. $35-$65.

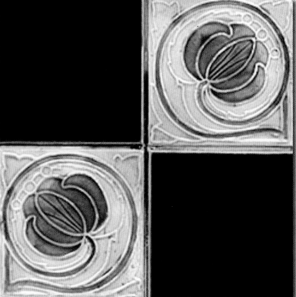

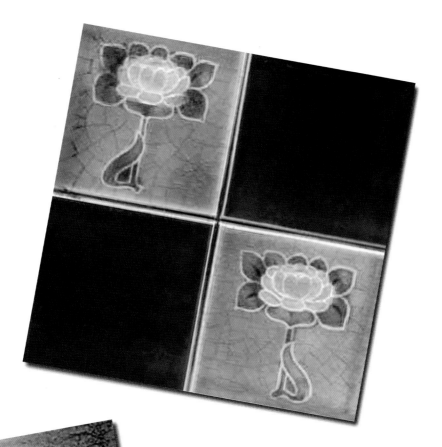

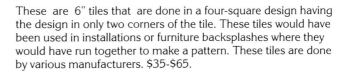

These are 6" tiles that are done in a four-square design having the design in only two corners of the tile. These tiles would have been used in installations or furniture backsplashes where they would have run together to make a pattern. These tiles are done by various manufacturers. $35-$65.

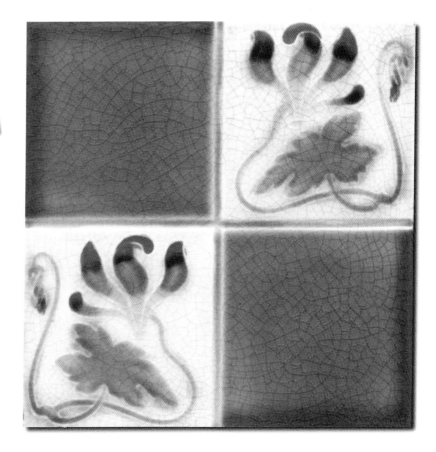

Transfer Tiles by Various Makers

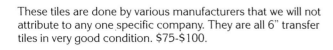

These tiles are done by various manufacturers that we will not attribute to any one specific company. They are all 6" transfer tiles in very good condition. $75-$100.

These tiles are done by various manufacturers that we will not attribute to any one specific company. They are all 6" transfer tiles in very good condition. $75-$100.

This is a 6" transfer tile done by Maw & Company. Very good condition. $100.

This is a 6" transfer tile done by H. Richards. Very good condition. $100.

This is a 6" transfer tile done by Pilkingtons Tile & Pottery Company, Ltd. Very good condition. $100.

Water Lily Tiles

Water Lily tiles done by various tile makers, c1890-1914. This was a very popular motif on tiles in this time frame and all of the companies had their own version of this flowing plant life. There are some very beautiful designs with great color glaze combinations.

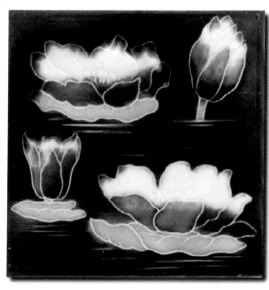

All of these tiles in this section will depict the ever popular water lily motif done on so many of the Art Nouveau Tiles. These are all 6" tiles in good condition done by various tile manufacturers. Note the same tiles done in different color combinations. $100-$135.

A 6" tile with water lily design. We believe that this is a French manufacturer. $100-$135.

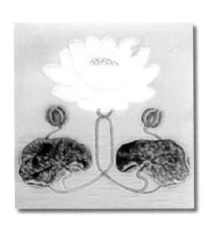

These are 6" tiles done by various German manufacturers. Good condition. $100-$135.

These are all 3" x 6" spacer tiles that would have run in a design on the horizontal. They are done by various unidentified manufacturers. $25-$75.

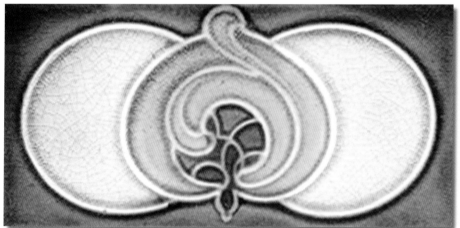

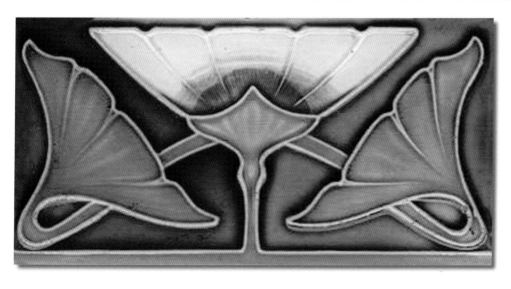

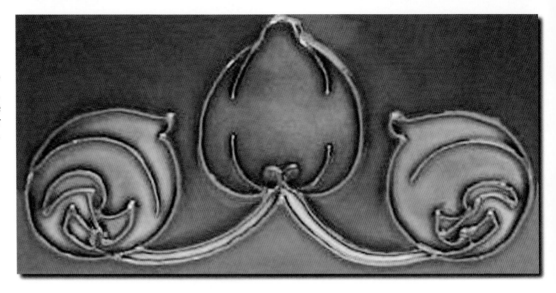

This is a beautiful 3" x 6" half tile done by W.E. Corn Brothers. Note the strong color combinations. $75.

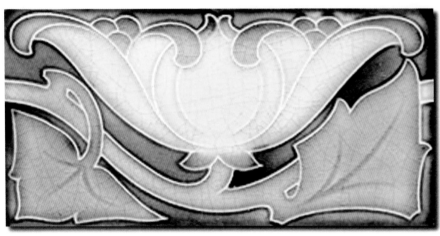

Here is an example of a half tile or spacer tile done by Pilkingtons Tile & Pottery Company, Ltd. This is an ultimate design that any Art Nouveau collector would want to add to their collection. $75-$100.

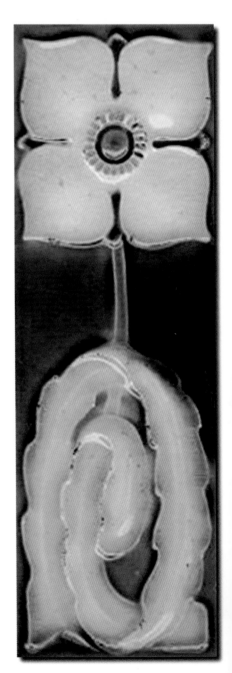

This is a really lovely 2" x 6" tile done by an unidentified maker. $65.

These tiles measure 3" x 3". The first is done by Pilkingtons Tile & Pottery Company, Ltd. The others are from unidentified manufacturers. $25-$45.

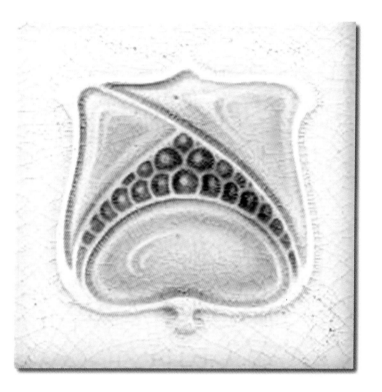

German Tiles

A really beautiful tile done by Johann von Schwarz of Nürnberg, Germany. This tile measures approximately 6" x 9". It is extremely well executed and of high quality. Designed by Carl Siegmund Luber about 1900. Tiles of this type are extremely rare and because of this will command a premium price.

These are all 6" tiles done by various German manufacturers. Notice the abstract lines in many of the designs. Note the strong and bold color combinations used in their glazes. The price range for these tiles in good condition is $100 -$150.

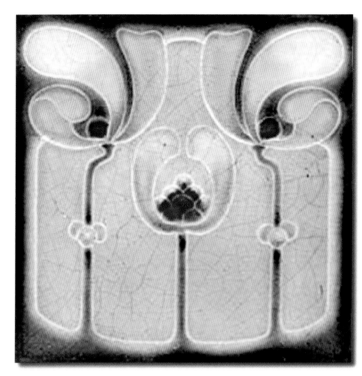

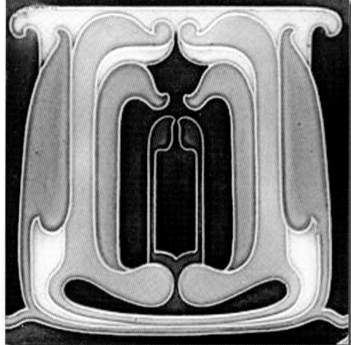

These are all 6" tiles done by various German manufacturers. Notice the abstract lines in many of the designs. Note the strong and bold color combinations used in their glazes. The price range for these tiles in good condition is $100 -$150.

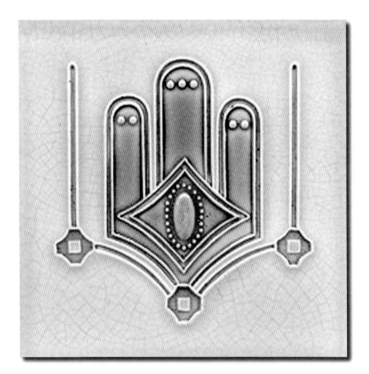

These are all 6" tiles done by various German manufacturers. Notice the abstract lines in many of the designs. Note the strong and bold color combinations used in their glazes. The price range for these tiles in good condition is $100 -$150.

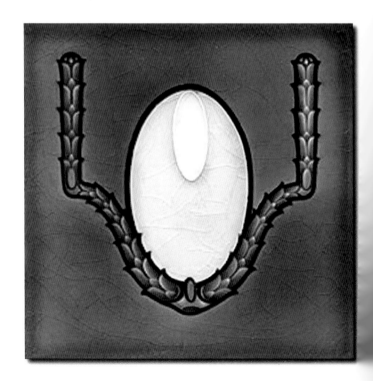

These are all 6" tiles done by various German manufacturers. Notice the abstract lines in many of the designs. Note the strong and bold color combinations used in their glazes. The price range for these tiles in good condition is $100 -$150.

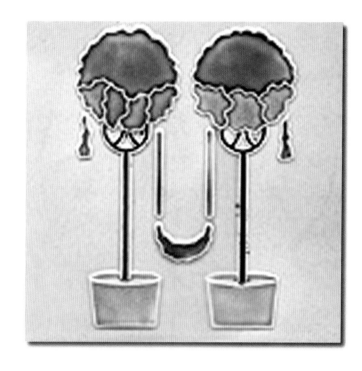

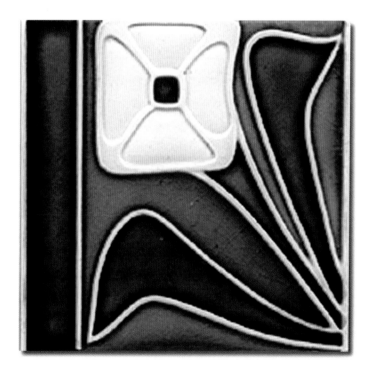

These are all 6" tiles done by various German manufacturers. Notice the abstract lines in many of the designs. Note the strong and bold color combinations used in their glazes. The price range for these tiles in good condition is $100 -$150.

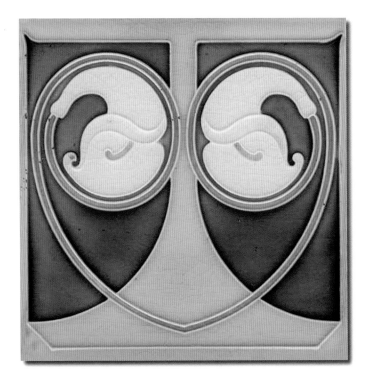

These are all 6" tiles done by various German manufacturers. Notice the abstract lines in many of the designs. Note the strong and bold color combinations used in their glazes. The price range for these tiles in good condition is $100 -$150.

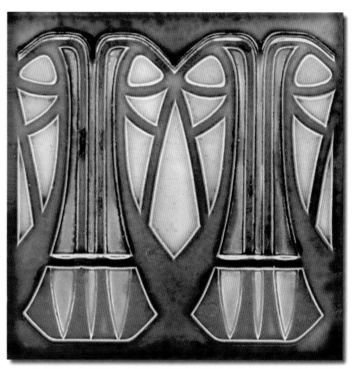

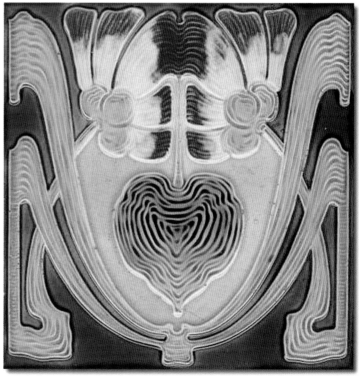

These are all 6" tiles done by various German manufacturers. Notice the abstract lines in many of the designs. Note the strong and bold color combinations used in their glazes. The price range for these tiles in good condition is $100 -$150.

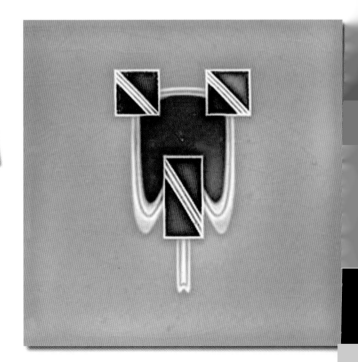

These are all 6" tiles done by various German manufacturers. Notice the abstract lines in many of the designs. Note the strong and bold color combinations used in their glazes. The price range for these tiles in good condition is $100 -$150.

Belgium Tiles

These are all 6" tiles done by various Belgium manufacturers. $100-$135

These are all 6" tiles done by various Belgium manufacturers. $100-$135

These are all 6" tiles done by various Belgium manufacturers. $100-$135

186

These are all 6" tiles done by various Belgium manufacturers. $100-$135

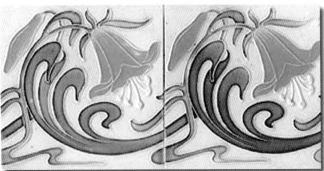

These are all 6" tiles done by unnamed Belgium manufacturers. $100-$135. Note how they were meant to flow in a continuous pattern.

These are all 6" tiles done by unnamed Belgium manufacturers. $100-$135. Note how they were meant to flow in a continuous pattern.

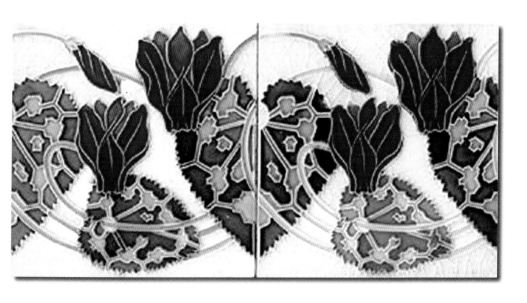

These are all 6" tiles done by
unnamed Belgium manufacturers.
$100-$135. Note how they were
meant to flow in a continuous
pattern.

Bibliography

Austwick, J & B. *The Decorated Tile: An Illustrated History of English Tile-making and Design*. Don Mills, Ontario, Canada: Collier Macmillian Canada, Ltd., 1980

Baeck, Mario & Verbrugge, Bart. DeBelgische *Art Nouveau Art Deco Wandtegels: 1880-1940*. Brussels, Belgium: Ministerie Van de Vlaamse Gemeenschap, 1996

Barnard, Julian. *Victorian Ceramic Tiles*. London, UK: Studio Vista/Christie's, 1972

Jullian, Philippe. *The Triumph of Art Nouveau: Paris Exhibition 1900*. New York, NY: Larousse & Co., Inc., 1974

Klamkin, Marian. *The Collector's Book of Art Nouveau*. New York, NY: Dodd, Mead & Co., 1971

Lemmen, Hans van. *Tiles: 1000 Years of Architectural Decoration*. New York, NY: Harry N. Abrams, Inc., 1993

Lemmen, Hans van & Malam, John, ed., *Fired Earth: 1,000 Years Of Tiles in Europe*. Shepton Beauchamp, Somerset, UK: Richard Dennis Publications, 1991

Lemmen, Hans van & Verbrugge, Bart. *Art Nouveau Tiles*. New York, NY: Rizzoli International Publications, Inc., 1999

Lockett, Terence A. *Collecting Victorian Tiles*. Woodbridge, Suffolk, UK: Antique Collectors' Club, 1979

Newbery, Elizabeth. *Art Nouveau: The Pitkin Guide*. Andover, Hampshire, UK: Pitkin Unichrome, Ltd., 2000

Riley, Noël. *Tile Art: A History of Decorative Ceramic Tiles*. Secaucus, N.J., Quintet Publishing Ltd., 1987

Schmutzler, Robert. *Art Nouveau*. New York, NY: Harry N. Abrams, Inc., 1978

Simmermacher, Rene. *Jugendstil-Fliesen*. Karlsruhe, Germany: Badisches Landesmuseum, 2000

Weisberg, Gabriel P. *Art Nouveau Bing: Paris Style 1900*. New York, NY: Harry N. Abrams, Inc., 1986

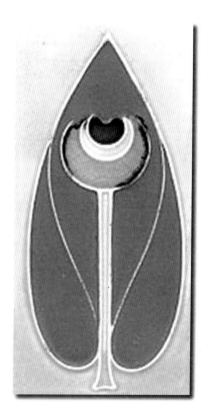

Organizations

American Art Pottery Association
    Secretary, JAAPA
    PO Box 1226
    Westport, MA 02790
Friends of Terra Cotta
    c/o Susan Tunick
    771 West End Ave., #10E
    New York, NY 10025
    212 932-1750
Tiles and Architectural Ceramics Society
    Decorative Arts Department
    Liverpool Museum
    William Brown St.
    Liverpool, L3 8EN
Tile Heritage Foundation
    PO Box 1850
    Healdsburg, CA 95448
    707 431-8453